Orlando

by Emma Stanford

Emma Stanford has written books and articles
on Florida, California, the Caribbean, Hawaii,
France and Spain, as well as Mediterranean
port guides for the US navy. She has also
contributed to guides published by the BTA,
American Express and Fodors.

Above: *Cooling off at Wet 'n Wild*

AA Publishing

Live at Gatorland

Written by Emma Stanford
Updated by Gary McKechnie

First published 1998.
Reprinted June and October 1999.
Reprinted April 2000.
Revised second edition 2001.
Reprinted June 2001.
Reprinted March, June and October 2002.
Reprinted 2004. Information verified and updated.
Reprinted April 2004. Reprinted May, Aug and Dec 2004.
Reprinted May 2005.
This edition 2006. Information verified and updated.

Published by AA Publishing, a trading name of Automobile
Association Developments Limited, whose registered office
is Fanum House, Basing View, Basingstoke, Hampshire
RG21 4EA.
Registered number 1878835.

Find out more about
AA Publishing and the
wide range of travel
publications and services
the AA provides by
visiting our website at
www.theAA.com/
bookshop

A02352
Atlas section and cover maps produced from
map data supplied by Global Mapping, Brackley,
UK
© Global Mapping

Colour separation: Keenes, Andover
Printed and bound in Italy by Printers Trento S.r.l.

Contents

About this Book

This book is divided into five sections to cover the most important aspects of your visit to Orlando.

Viewing Orlando pages 5–14
An introduction to Orlando by the author.
Orlando's Features
Essence of Orlando
The Shaping of Orlando
Peace and Quiet
Orlando's Famous

Top Ten pages 15–26
The author's choice of the Top Ten places to see in and around Orlando, each with practical information.

What to See pages 27–90
The three main areas in and around Orlando, each with its own brief introduction and an alphabetical listing of the main attractions.
Practical information
Snippets of "Did You Know…" information
5 suggested tours
2 features

Where To… pages 91–116
Detailed listings of the best places to eat, stay, shop, take the children and be entertained.

Practical Matters pages 117–24
A highly visual section containing essential travel information.

Maps
All map references are to the individual maps found in the What to See section of this guide.
For example, Busch Gardens has the reference ✚ 46A1—indicating the page on which the map is located and the grid square in which the attraction is to be found. A list of the maps that have been used in this travel guide can be found in the index.

Prices
Where appropriate, an indication of the cost of an establishment is given by **$** signs:
$$$** denotes higher prices, **$$** denotes average prices, while **$ denotes lower charges.

Star Ratings
Most of the places described in this book have been given a separate rating:
✪✪✪ Do not miss
✪✪ Highly recommended
✪ Worth seeing

Viewing
Orlando

Above: *Face-painting at Lake Eola Park*
Right: *Southern belle, Cypress Gardens*

Emma Stanford's Orlando

Dolphins working out at SeaWorld Orlando

Getting Around

Short-stay visitors can tackle Orlando without a car, though public transportation is pretty sketchy. Most hotels offer free shuttles to Walt Disney World, and Orlando's International Drive resort area has the inexpensive and efficient I-Ride trolley bus (7am– midnight, stopping every two blocks in the 8 miles (13km) between SeaWorld Orlando and Belz Factory Outlet mall). For longer stays, independent transportation is a worthwhile investment, opening up a host of alternative day trips to the Gulf coast or Atlantic beaches, state parks and other Central Florida attractions.

Orlando really is the town that Mickey Mouse built. A former cattle ranchers' watering hole and citrus depot in dusty Central Florida, the quiet country town boomed after the opening of the first Walt Disney World theme park, Magic Kingdom, in 1971. Today, Orlando is firmly established as one of the world's top vacation destinations.

Some 43 million visitors pour into Orlando every year; over the past quarter century, over 500 million have visited Walt Disney World Resort. The sheer volume of interest in Orlando has meant that the city has grown fast—often too fast for developers to concern themselves with the niceties of landscaping or public transportation—and the main tourist areas have spread out well beyond Orlando itself. Many visitors to Walt Disney World Resort, a 30-minute drive south of heavily touristed International Drive, choose to stay in the neighboring town of Kissimmee. However, what Orlando may lack in aesthetic urban planning it more than makes up for in thrills and Disney magic. This is theme park heaven, boasting state-of-the-art rides, family entertainment and fantasy on tap. Add high standards of service and you have a vacation destination that could teach the rest of the world a thing or two.

Orlando's Features

Distances
• Distance from Miami: 236 miles (381km)
• Distance from New York: 944 miles (1,522km)
• Distance from Los Angeles: 2,203 miles (3,553km)
• Distance from London: 4,336 miles (6,994km)

Size
• Population: 180,500 (City of Orlando); 1.6 million (Greater Orlando)
• Population density: 4,000 people per square mile
• Annual visitors: 43 million

Geography
• Latitude: N 28° 32'
• Longitude: W 81° 22'
• Height above sea level: 70ft (21m)

Climate
• Warmest months: July–August (high 92°F/33°C, low 73°F/23°C)
• Coolest month: January (high 72°F/22°C, low 49°F/9°C)
• Wettest month: July (7.8in/20cm of rain)
• Driest months: November–December (1.8in/5cm of rain)

Top: *The Orlando skyline*
Above: *Catching the surf on the Atlantic coast*

Facilities
• Hotel rooms: 114,000
• Restaurants: 4,500-plus
• Visitor attractions: approximately 100
• Golf courses: 150-plus
• Watersports: 300-plus inland lakes, springs and rivers for fishing, swimming and boating; an hour's drive from the Atlantic and Gulf coasts
• Spectator sports: basketball (Orlando Magic and Women's NBA team, Orlando Miracle); baseball (Orlando Rays and spring training visitors, the Atlanta Braves and Houston Astros); American football (Orlando Predators)
• Retail shopping space: 52 million sq ft (5 million sq m)
• Transport: Orlando International Airport is the 16th busiest in the US (28th in the world), with around 700 flights daily serving more than 100 cities worldwide.

As You Like It
There are two versions of how Orlando came to be named. One credits pioneer settler and local big-wig, Judge V. D. Speer, with having named the town after a character in his favorite Shakespeare play, *As You Like It*. The other is that the town was named after Orlando Reeves, a US soldier killed by an Indian arrow in 1835 while raising the alarm to save his company, in what is now downtown Orlando's Lake Eola Park.

Essence of Orlando

Below: *Woody Woodpecker, a favorite with younger guests*
Bottom: *Fun on the rapids at Busch Gardens*

The essence of Orlando is entertainment. From the tips of Disney-MGM Studios' Earffel Tower down to the sandy bunkers of more than 100 golf courses, Orlando is a full-on, year-round crowd pleaser. Visitors can share their breakfast muffins with Goofy and the gang, get whisked aboard a Magic Carpet at the Arabian Nights dinner theater and never really set foot in Florida. But this would be a mistake. Beyond the man-made wonders, Central Florida offers sparkling lakes, citrus groves, lovely gardens and a rich and varied wildlife showcased in relaxing state parks.

THE 10 ESSENTIALS

If you only have a short time to visit Orlando, or would like to get a really complete picture of the region, here are the essentials:

• **Magic Kingdom:** the "must see" classic Disney park (➤ 84–7).

• **Amazing Adventures of Spider-Man:** Islands of Adventure's incredible blend of indoor fireworks, villains, virtual reality and unbelievably surreal sensations makes this a must-see.

• **Manatees,** or sea cows, are the endangered gentle giants of Florida's waterways. If you cannot get to see them in the wild (➤ 51), do not miss SeaWorld's Manatees: The Last Generation? (➤ 36).

• **Do the birdwalk,** a little-known secret: the Gatorland marsh boardwalk is one of the best birdwatching spots in the region (➤ 32).

• **Blooming marvellous:** for local horticultural color, enjoy the formal delights of the Harry P. Leu Gardens (➤ 33), or the woodland trails of Bok Tower Gardens (➤ 47).

• **Silver Spurs:** cattle ranchers first settled the area in the 1840s and Kissimmee celebrates its origins with the biannual Silver Spurs Rodeo (➤ 60).

• **Drink up!** Florida produces around 75 percent of the nation's citrus crop, so be sure to sample fresh local juices.

• **Shop 'til you drop:** the top end of Orlando's International Drive has turned into a magnet for bargain-hunters, with factory outlet stores galore (➤ 105).

• **Look into the future:** forget sci-fi for a moment and head "Behind the Seeds" at Disney's Epcot Center for a fascinating look at the future of agriculture (➤ 81).

• **Doing dinner** can be quite an event in Orlando. A host of popular dinner theaters offers themed evenings from Medieval Times to 1930s-style Capone's (➤ 113).

Above: *Fresh Florida oranges*
Below: *Shoppers flock to Orlando's bargain desinger outlets*

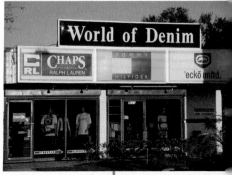

The Shaping of Orlando

Spanish explorer Juan Ponce de León found Florida while looking for the fountain of youth

1513
Spanish explorer Juan Ponce de León discovers Florida.

1565
Pedro Menéndez de Avilés, Captain General of the Spanish treasure fleets, founds St. Augustine on the Atlantic coast, the oldest continuously inhabited European settlement in the US.

10

1763–83
The British occupy Florida for 20 years before it is returned to Spain under the Second Treaty of Paris.

1817–18
Tensions between the incoming white settlers and native American Seminole Indians spark the First Seminole War.

1819
Spain relinquishes Florida to the US in settlement of a $5 million debt.

1835–42
Second Seminole War. Fort Gatlin established close to present-day Orlando c1837.

1842
The US army escorts 3,000 Seminole Indians on the "Trail of Tears" to exile on reservations west of the Mississippi. Settlers move into Central Florida.

1843
Cattleman pioneer Aaron Jernigan arrives from Georgia, and constructs a stockade on the shores of Lake Holden. The early settlement in the vicinity of Fort Gatlin is named Jernigan in 1850.

1845
Florida achieves statehood.

1857
Jernigan is renamed Orlando (see panel on ➤ 7). Local settlers make their living from cattle-ranching and cotton.

1861
Florida is the third state to secede from the Union and join the Confederacy. Start of the Civil War (1861–5).

1865
W. H. Holden plants Orlando's first

commercial citrus plantation on his 100-acre (40-ha) property. At first the fruit has to be hauled overland to Sanford and then carried by boat to markets in Charleston, South Carolina.

1875
The City of Orlando (all 2sq miles/5sq km of it), county seat of Orange County, is officially incorporated by a vote of 22 men from the total population of 85.

1880
Henry Plant's South Florida Railroad links Kissimmee/Orlando to Tampa on the Gulf coast.

1890s
English settlers buy up land around Orlando for around $1 an acre and plant citrus.

1894–5
The Great Freeze devastates Central Florida's citrus groves. Faced with ruin, the English settlers are rumored to have consoled themselves by playing cricket. Meanwhile, orange-grower John B. Steinmetz converts his packing house into a skating rink with picnic facilities, a toboggan slide and a bath house, creating Orlando's first visitor attraction.

1922
First cargo planes land at Orlando, followed by passengers in 1928.

1929
Mediterranean fruit fly attacks citrus orchards in the Orlando area. The National Guard are called out to enforce quarantine regulations and spray the infected crop, and the threat is eradicated within a year.

1956
The Glenn L. Martin Company of Baltimore (now Lockheed Martin) annouces plans to build a missile factory in Orange County, giving a considerable boost to the local economy, together with the proximity of the new Cape Canaveral aerospace complex.

1965
Walt Disney announces his plans for Walt Disney World.

1971
The first phase of Walt Disney World, Magic Kingdom, opens.

1977
The last orange grove on Orlando's famous Orange Avenue is bulldozed to make way for a shopping center.

1982
Epcot Center opens.

1989
Disney–MGM Studios opens. The three Walt Disney World theme parks comprise the world's number one tourist destination.

1990
Universal Studios opens.

1998
Walt Disney World opens Disney's Animal Kingdom, its fourth full-size theme park.

1999
Universal Studios unveils a second theme park, Islands of Adventure, and a full vacation resort complex.

The space shuttle Discovery taking off

11

Peace & Quiet

Escaping the hustle and bustle of Orlando's theme parks and non-stop fun is not only an attractive idea but essential if you are spending more than a few days in town. Though Central Florida is not renowned for its scenery—undulating citrus groves are the main feature—it is remarkably easy to step back from the concrete jungle and discover pockets of wild, undeveloped natural Florida just around the corner.

Below: *Canoeists in Weikiwa Springs State Park*
Inset: *A limpkin in the Wakulla Springs State Park*

Water, Water Everywhere

There are more than 300 named lakes and dozens of rivers, ponds and springs in the vicinity of Orlando, offering excellent bass-fishing, boating and swimming opportunities. They also act as a magnet for wildlife, particularly waterbirds such as herons, snowy egrets, coots, gallinules and the bizarre-looking anhinga bird, which swims with its body beneath the surface and only its long, thin, snake-like neck protruding, hence its nickname 'snakebird.'

A boat tour of Lake Tohopekaliga, in Kissimmee, is a great way to get away from it all, and there is a good chance of spotting bald eagles and osprey, as well as more common species. Tours depart from the marina and there are boats and fishing tackle for hire (► 61). There are also scenic boat trips on Winter Park's lakes, where wildlife plays second string to expensive lakeshore real estate, but the odd alligator occasionally surfaces to give passengers a thrill for their money (► 67).

Nature Trails

Within easy reach of Orlando, there are more than half-a-dozen state parks giving access to unspoilt wilderness, marshland boardwalks and nature trails for wildlife-spotting, as well as canoe runs, fishing lakes and picnic grounds in a natural setting. North of Orlando, the sand pine woods of Ocala National Forest are one of the last refuges of the

A colorful shrub in Fairchild Tropical Gardens

Florida black bear and home to barred owls and wild turkeys. A 66-mile (106-km) section of the cross-state Florida National Scenic Trail runs through the forest, and there are numerous shorter trails, while canoe runs such

as Juniper Springs are reckoned to be among the best in the state (► 62).

For winter visitors to picturesque Blue Spring State Park, on the St. John's River, there is the added incentive of spotting a manatee (► 51). You could combine a nature walk with a visit to the beach on a day trip to Merritt Island National Wildlife Refuge and the Canaveral National Seashore, in the shadow of the Kennedy Space Center launch pad on the Atlantic Coast (► 58).

Glorious Gardens

If nature in the raw does not appeal, there is peace and quiet to be found in a brace of delightful gardens. Just north of downtown, Harry P. Leu Gardens is a tranquil lakeshore spot boasting one of the finest camellia collections in the US (► 33). The shady woodlands of Bok Tower Gardens, near Lake Wales, make a soothing escape, where the only sound to disturb the birdsong is the chimes of the famous carillon (► 47).

Orlando's Famous

Osceola, champion of the Seminoles, pictured in about 1830

Osceola

A charismatic warrior and the principal native American leader of the Second Seminole War, Osceola (c1803–38) settled near the Peace River south of Orlando in around 1808. Utterly opposed to the forced migration of Seminole Indians to reservations west of the Mississippi, Osceola's hostility towards white settlers and the US government was further inflamed by the kidnap of his wife, Che-cho-ter (Morning Dew), whose trace of Negro blood allowed her white captors to claim she was a fugitive slave. After executing a Miccosukee chief for accepting government money to migrate, Osceola led an attack on Fort King which triggered the outbreak of war in 1835. Public outcry greeted Osceola's unlawful capture while negotiating under a flag of truce in 1837, but he was held in St. Augustine and transferred to Fort Moultrie, South Carolina, where he died.

Zora Neale Hurston

Celebrated Black folklorist and writer Zora Neale Hurston (1903–60), was born and raised north of Orlando, in Eatonville, one of the first incorporated Negro towns in the US. Employing the language of the rural Black south, she wrote evocatively of her people. Her mostly widely acclaimed novel, *Their Eyes Were Watching God*, was published in 1937, and an autobiography, *Dust Tracks on a Road*, in 1942. See also ► 69.

Mickey Mouse

Mickey Mouse was born in California in 1928 (► panel). He made his first screen appearance that year in *Steamboat Willie*, and went on to star in more than 100 cartoon movies, including a challenging role as the Sorcerer's Apprentice in *Fantasia* (1940). Mickey and his companion, Minnie, established a base in Florida in 1971 and also have homes in France and Japan.

A Star is Born
As a teenager living in Kansas, the man behind the Mouse, Walter Elias Disney (1901–66), took a correspondence course in cartoon-drawing. When a successful early cartoon character, Oswald the Lucky Rabbit, fell victim to an unscrupulous distributor, Disney returned to the drawing board and created Mortimer Mouse, inspired, so the story goes, by the field mice that used to frequent his old Kansas City studio. The mouse was renamed Mickey by Disney's wife, Lillian. The rest is history.

Top Ten

Above: *Whale at SeaWorld Orlando*
Right: *Posing at Kennedy Space Center*

15

1
Busch Gardens

Hold on for a stomach-churning ride

The combination of exotic animals, thrilling roller-coasters, water rides and shows makes this one of Florida's top attractions.

Busch Gardens lies around 75 minutes' drive west of Orlando, in Tampa. Opened in 1959, it is a seasoned crowd-pleaser with pleasantly mature grounds shaded by trees and flowering shrubs. The overall plot is "Africa," with 10 themed areas such as Nairobi, Timbuktu and the Serengeti Plain; the latter incorporates the interactive Edge of Africa domain, inaugurated in the summer of 1997.

The 350-acre (141-ha) park houses one of the nation's premier zoos. There are more than 2,000 animals from over 300 species wandering the grassland enclosures of the Serengeti Plain, inhabiting the rocks and waterfalls of the Great Ape Domain and featured in other displays such as the Bird Gardens. Busch Gardens plays a significant role in breeding and conserving endangered species and many of the zoo's latest additions are proudly displayed in the Nairobi Animal Nursery.

But animals are by no means all the park has to offer: roller-coaster fans are also in for a big treat. Check out the duelling, double wooden roller-coaster Gwazi and Montu, one of the tallest and longest inverted coasters in the world. The Kumba ride remains among the largest and fastest steel roller-coasters in existence, and assorted water rides provide varying degrees of thrills and spills, plus a chance to cool off in the Florida sunshine.

Small children are particularly well catered-for here. In addition to the animal attractions, there is the interactive Land of the Dragons play area, and colorful "Lion King" style show in the Moroccan Palace Theater. Strollers are available for rental in the Morocco district and there is a full baby-changing and nursing area in Land of the Dragons.

See also ➤ 48–50.

www.buschgardens.com

✚ Off map 46A1

✉ Busch Boulevard, Tampa (75 miles/121km west of Orlando via I-4 West and I-75 North to Fowler Avenue/Exit 54)

☎ (813) 987 5082 or 1-888 800 5447

🕐 Daily 10–6 (extended summer and hols)

🍴 Refreshment stops throughout park, plus the full-service Crown Colony Restaurant (Crown Colony) ($–$$)

♿ Very good

💰 Very expensive

❓ Check daily schedules for show times

2

Cypress Gardens Adventure Park

Florida's first theme park remains faithful to its botanical origins and is famous for its four annual flower festivals.

Sloping gently down to the shores of Lake Eloise, near Winter Haven, a 45-minute drive south of Orlando, Cypress Gardens was originally laid out in the 1930s along the swampy water's edge, shaded by giant cypress trees. The park has expanded considerably since, covering more than 220 acres (89ha), and offers a variety of shows, shopping, dining and animal attractions in addition to the carefully manicured gardens, eye-catching topiary and other horticultural exhibits.

For plant-lovers, the lush Botanical Gardens remain the highlight of a visit. Shaded brick paths meander through dense tropical plantings of heliconias and bromeliads, cascades of brilliantly colored bougainvillea and forests of bamboo. There are acres of formal gardens, too.

But flower power aside, Cypress Gardens takes pride in its water-ski revues on the lake, and the 153-ft (47-m) high Island in the Sky revolving observatory. At its foot, Jubilee Junction houses snack stops, restaurants and shops.

Other attractions concentrate on the wonders of the natural world, with the Butterfly Conservatory and the Nature's Way area featuring animal enclosures and a wooden boardwalk area on the lake. A recent addition is a kid-pleasing assortment of amusement rides: tilt-a-whirls, roller coasters, flume rides, and other cars and cages that flip, spin and roll. To be sure, however, this is still a botanical garden at heart and a good place to experience an old-fashioned Florida attraction. See also ► 52.

✚ 46B1

✉ SR540 West 4 miles (6.5km) east of Winter Haven, off US27, 22 miles (35km) south of I-4

☎ (863) 324 2111

🕐 Daily 10–6 (extended for hols and special events)

🍴 Aunt Julie's Country Kitchen ($–$$); Backwater Bill's BBQ ($); Gator Bites ($); Village Fare Food Court ($); assorted snack and refreshment stops ($)

♿ Very good

✋ Very expensive

↔ Bok Tower Gardens (► 47), Lake Wales (► 61)

Cypress Gardens, colorful at any time of the year

17

3
Discovery Cove

www.discoverycove.com

✚ 29B2

✉ 6000 Discovery Cove Way (1-4/Exit 71 or 72)

☎ (407) 370 1280 or 1-877 434 7268

🕐 Daily 9–5.30

🍴 Lunch in the Laguna Grill is included in the admission price; the Oasis snack cabanas ($) serve refreshments

🚌 I-Ride, Lynx #42

Swim with dolphins, rays and thousands of tropical fish then laze on the sand at this beach paradise created in landlocked Orlando.

To swim with dolphins is a cherished dream for millions of animal lovers worldwide, so it should come as no surprise that somebody in Orlando came up with the brilliant idea of creating a theme park where this particular dream can come true. Sister to the world-famous SeaWorld Orlando (▶ 21, 36–37) theme park across the road (and Busch Gardens in Tampa, ▶ 16, 48–50), Discovery Cove opened its doors in 2000 and has been so successful that the park has just completed its first major expansion program. Unlike other theme parks, which rely on a high turnover of guests, Discovery Cove aims for exclusivity. Admission is by advance reservation only and limited to 1,000 guests

Meeting a dolphin

♿ Very good, includes wheelchairs adapted for sandy beaches

✋ Very expensive; a reduced package is available for children 3–5 and guests who do not take part in the dolphin swim

❓ The hands-on Trainer for a Day program is available for up to 12 guests a day. Reservations essential

per day ensuring the park is never over-run and the all-important dolphin-swim program is not compromised. The all-inclusive tickets include a personal guide, unlimited access to all swim and snorkeling areas, the use of snorkel equipment, wetsuits, towels, lockers and beach chairs, plus a freshly prepared meal and a seven-day unlimited use pass to neighboring SeaWorld Orlando.

The highlight of the day is undoubtedly the 45-minute dolphin swim (30 minutes of which are spent in the water though guests need not be strong swimmers), yet there is plenty more to see and do. Don a snorkel to explore a colorful manmade reef teeming with tropical fish and swim in the Ray Lagoon, then take time out on dry land to bask on the beach or visit the huge, free-flight aviary.

See also ▶ 30.

4
Fantasy of Flight

Vintage planes, each with a story to tell, help illustrate aviation history at this Central Florida aviation attraction.

The first thing to notice at Fantasy of Flight is the elegant 1930s and 1940s-style art deco themed buildings, designed to capture the spirit of aviation's Golden Era. Within the twin hangars and parked out on the runways are more than 20 vintage aircraft, just a part of the world's largest private collection built up over the last quarter century by aviation enthusiast Kermit Weeks.

The earliest authentic aircraft on display here, including a Sopwith Camel, date from World War I. However, illustrating the real dawn of flight, there is a reproduction of the Wright Brothers' 1903 Kitty Hawk Flyer, a cat's-cradle of wires and wooden struts, which has actually flown—if only for a few seconds at a time. A prime Golden Era exhibit with a notable history is the 1929 Ford Tri-Motor, launched by movie star Gloria Swanson. It flew across the US coast-to-coast in 48 hours and was later used in the making of *Indiana Jones and the Temple of Doom*.

The collection of World War II fighter planes from the US, Britain and Germany are among the museum's most popular exhibits, and visitors can test out their air combat skills in the Fightertown Flight Simulators, piloting their way through an aerial dogfight over the Pacific. Another themed "immersion experience" is the History of Flight, which features walk-through dioramas. Backlot Tours take visitors behind the scenes to see the restoration workshops (weather permitting).

See also ➤ 53.

✚ 46A1

✉ SR559, Polk City (I-4 West to Exit 44)

☎ (863) 984 3500

🕐 Daily 9–5

🍴 Compass Rose ($–$$)

♿ Good

✋ Expensive

❓ Call for details of hot air balloon and biplane rides

Fantasy of Flight, where the past comes to life

5
Kennedy Space Center

www.kennedyspacecenter.
com

✚ 47D2

✉ SR405, Merritt Island
(Bee Line
Expressway/SR528 toll
road east from Orlando)

☎ (321) 449 4444 or (321)
454 4198 TDD

🕐 Daily 9–dusk

🍴 Mila's ($–$$); cafés and
concessions ($)

♿ Very good

✋ Expensive

❓ Bus tours depart
regularly (allow 2½
hours).

*Tours, films, rockets and space hardware bring the
American space program to life at NASA's Florida
space launch facility.*

The Kennedy Space Center Visitor Complex is the gateway
to Launch Complex 39, where space shuttles will one day
again blast off into orbit, and where Apollo 11 set off on its
ground-breaking journey to deliver the first man to walk on
the moon in 1969. A visit to the Space Center offers a
terrific opportunity to delve into the history of the US space
program, experience a nail-biting re-creation of the
countdown to blast off, get a behind-the-scenes view of
space technology and look at the shape of things to come.

The very first rockets launched from Cape Canaveral
were long-range guided missiles fired from Cape Canaveral
Air Force Station in the early 1950s. NASA, the National
Aeronautics and Space Administration established in 1958
to carry out the peaceful exploration and use of space,
later used the site to prepare and launch science satellites
and the manned and unmanned flights of the early
Mercury and Gemini programs. In 1964, NASA transferred
operations to Launch Complex 39, at Merritt Island, which
was designed to handle the Apollo-Saturn V program. The
first launch from the
Kennedy Space Center
was the Apollo 8 mission
December 1968.

Today, bus tours offer
views of the shuttle launch
pads, the gargantuan
Vehicle Assembly Building
(VAB) and make a stop at
the spectacular $37-million
Apollo/Saturn V Center,
which features an actual,
unused, Saturn V rocket.
Families with small
children will find a half-day
visit long enough. But do
save time to watch at least
one Imax movie (included
in admission). "The Dream
is Alive" and "Space
Station 3–D" are inspiring.
See also ➤ 59.

*The Space Shuttle exhibit
comes highly recommended*

6
SeaWorld Orlando

Shamu, the killer whale, star of SeaWorld, heads up an all-star cast at the world's most popular sea life park.

A walrus steals the show at SeaWorld

Laid out over an action-packed 200-acre (81-ha) site, SeaWorld provides a full day's itinerary of shows and marine encounters in the best theme park tradition. The stars of the shows are almost exclusively of the finned or flippered variety and their virtuoso performances (coaxed by the strategic deployment of a seemingly endless supply of fish) are a source of continuous amazement and delight to packed audiences. Though SeaWorld can get very busy, its built-in advantage over other traditional parks is the scarcity of rides, so there are few long lines.

Shamu shows, especially the evening version—Shamu Rocks America—are hugely popular and performances in the Whale & Dolphin Stadium and the Sea Lion & Otter Stadium are a must. The Penguin Encounter (with real snow) should not be missed, and anybody who has never seen a manatee should rectify this immediately at Manatees: The Last Generation?.

SeaWorld pushes its role as a significant animal rescue, conservation and research facility. There are several entertaining and educational behind-the-scenes tours for interested guests as well as summer camp adventures. For an even more interactive experience, SeaWorld's sister park, Discovery Cove, invites guests to swim with bottlenose dolphins and tropical fish (➤ 17, 32).

See also ➤ 36–7

www.seaworld.com

46B2

7007 SeaWorld Drive, Orlando (I-4/Exit 71

(407) 351 3600

Daily 9–7 (extended summer and hols)

Makahiki Luau, Dine With Shamu, Sharks Underwater Grill ($$$), reservations ☎ 1-800 327 2424. Also assorted cafés, snack, BBQ and sandwich shops

I-Ride, Lynx #42

Very good

Very expensive. There is a 10 percent discount for ticket purchases made over the internet, or as part of the 4- and 5-Park Orlando Flex Tickets

21

7
Silver Springs

Boat trips, jeep safaris, animal encounters and popular music shows are all part of the deal at "Florida's Original Attraction."

All aboard the Silver Queen

www.silversprings.com

🔗 46A4

✉ SR40, 1 mile (1.61km) east of Ocala (72 miles/116km northwest of Orlando)

☎ (352) 236 2121 or 1-800 234 7458

🕐 Daily 10–5 (extended summer and hols)

🍴 The Deli ($); Springside Pizzeria ($); Springside Restaurant ($–$$); Swampy's Smokehouse Buffet ($–$$); snack stops, ice creams and cold drinks stalls ($)

♿ Good

💸 Very expensive

↔ Ocala National Forest (► 62)

In 1878, Silver Springs entrepreneur Hullam Jones had a brainwave. He installed a glass viewing box in the flat bottom of a dugout canoe and invented the glass-bottomed boat tour, hence this popular nature park's claim to being the Sunshine State's first tourist attraction.

More than a century on, the glass-bottomed boat rides are as popular as ever, creating a window into an under-water world teeming with fish, turtles, crustaceans and ancient fossils at the head of the world's largest artesian spring formation. You can also enjoy the Lost River Voyage that plies the unspoilt Silver River, with a stop at a wildlife rescue outpost; or a Jungle Cruise on Fort King Waterway, where non-native animals look on. Jeep safaris also do the jungle thing, four-wheeling through a 35-acre (14-ha) Florida jungle, with specially designed animal habitats like Big Gator Lagoon.

Showtime at Silver Springs brings on the bugs and the creepy-crawlies at Creature Feature, an alarmingly up-close look at spiders and scorpions, toads and giant Madagascan hissing cockroaches. For something a little more wholesome, watch domestic cats and dogs performing tricks at the Amazing Pets displays. The park also attracts popular music acts for its annual weekend Concert Series (included with admission) starting in March—the likes of Johnny Cash, Crystal Gayle and the Beach Boys have performed here. See also ► 63.

8
Wet 'n' Wild

If the beach is too far, Wet 'n' Wild is a perfect— and in some ways much more exciting—alternative

When it opened in 1977, Wet 'n' Wild set the standard for the elaborate water park. There was more than simply a few slides here; there were twisting, barreling, churning rapids as well as innovative watery rides, wide beaches, a surf lagoon, restaurants, picnic areas and a lazy river. The park, located on International Drive, is hugely popular from April to October, with the peak season running from June through August.

You will be astonished at the ingenuity that has gone into creating heart-stopping thrill rides. For instance, the Black Hole sends you shooting 500ft (152m) down a spinning, twisting, dark tunnel, forced through by a gusher of water. Blue Niagara is a 60-ft (18-m) tall twisted, twin water slide that shoots you down the pipe. One of the scariest attractions is Bomb Bay. Step into a large enclosed cylinder, cross your arms and legs, and then the floor below you drops out to send you sliding on a 76-ft (23-m) vertical free fall before you slip into a curve to slow your descent. Kids are catered to with a separate area featuring thrilling kid-sized rides and attractions.

You don't have to be a thrillseeker to enjoy Wet 'n' Wild; there are plenty of more peaceful offerings. You can bring picnic lunches and coolers with food into the park, the pools are heated, as many as 400 lifeguards are on duty in peak season, and this is one of the rare water parks opened year-round. See also ► 43.

✚ 29B2

✉ 6200 International Drive (1–4/Exit 75AB)

☎ (407) 351-1800 or 1-800 992-WILD

🕐 Daily 10–5 (extending 9–9 in summer)

🍴 Surf Grill ($–$$); Bubba's BBQ & Chicken ($–$$); Pizza & Subs ($–$$); Cookies & Cones ($)

♿ Good

✋ Very expensive

↔ Universal Orlando (► 26, 38–43)

Fun for all the family

23

9
Walt Disney World Resort

🕇 29A1

✉ Walt Disney World Resort, Lake Buena Vista (I-4/Exits 25-B and 26-B, 20 miles/32km south of Orlando)

☎ (407) 824 4321

🕐 Check current schedules

🍴 Each park offers a wide choice of dining options open for breakfast, lunch, dinner, and snacks throughout the day. Priority seating (☎ (407) 939 3463 or bookings service at Guest Relations) is advised for table service restaurants ($$–$$$)

🚌 Free shuttle bus services from many Orlando/Kissimmee hotels

♿ Excellent

✋ Very expensive

❓ Details of daily parades, showtimes and nighttime fireworks and laser displays are printed in current park guides. Tickets are available on a one-day, one-park basis. For longer stay guests, a choice of multi-day passes offer greater flexibility and savings. They cover unlimited admission to any combination of theme parks, WDW Resort transportation, and limited admission out to other Disney attractions such as the water parks, Pleasure Island, DisneyQuest and Disney's Wide World of Sports. Unused days never expire and can be used on a future visit.

This is the big one: Walt Disney's Florida showcase put Orlando on the map and has become a legend in its own short lifetime.

Walt Disney World Resort is the largest and most famous theme park resort in the world. Its 27,500-acre (11,134-ha) site is twice the size of Manhattan, and although only a small portion of this has been developed to date, it has four major theme parks: Magic Kingdom, Epcot, Disney-MGM Studios and Disney's Animal Kingdom, plus two water parks, a nightclub area within the huge lakefront Downtown Disney shopping, dining and entertainment district, themed resorts, gardens, lakes, championship golf courses and a professional sports complex.

Walt Disney opened his first theme park in Anaheim, California, in 1955. Disneyland, the prototype for the Magic Kingdom, which now flourishes in Japan, France and soon, Hong Kong, as well as Florida, was a huge success, but Disney was unable to control the explosion of hotels that popped up around the site and prevented him from expanding the park. Instead, he looked for alternative spots and was drawn to Orlando for its climate, communications links and vast tracts of cheap farmland, which he began to purchase in secret during 1964. With 27,500 acres (11,134ha) in the bag at a cost of about $5.5 million, Disney announced his plans to create "a complete vacation environment" unsullied by low rent commercialism.

Disney died in 1966 without seeing his Florida vision completed. But The Walt Disney Company did him proud, producing Magic Kingdom in Disneyland's image. This opened in 1971, followed by Epcot (Experimental Prototype Community Of Tomorrow), a futuristic pet project devised by Disney that finally opened in 1982. Disney-MGM Studios was rushed out in 1989, months ahead of Universal Studios' mammoth Florida facility (▶ 26); and now Central Florida's animal-orientated parks are feeling the pinch as Disney's Animal Kingdom exercises its powerful Disney appeal on the public.

"Doing Disney" is quite an undertaking. There is so much to see that it is all too easy to overdo things, and first-time visitors are in danger of wearing themselves out with ambitious plans to see the lot in a couple of days. Take a tip from the repeat visitors who plan their itineraries with almost military precision, zero in on the best rides and avoid the restaurants at peak times. Never plan on doing more than one park a day, and if you are visiting all four theme parks during your stay, include at least one rest day.

Cost is another important consideration: Disney does

not come cheap. If money is no object, Walt Disney World Resort is without doubt the best place to stay, with a choice of fine hotels boasting excellent facilities and free transport to the parks. Package deals paid in advance to cover theme park tickets and accommodations in Walt Disney World Resort hotels are one way of avoiding a nasty shock. For budget travelers there is plenty of affordable accommodations nearby in Kissimmee, or around Orlando's International Drive.

See also ➤ 70–90.

Cinderella Castle, Walt Disney World Resort's most famous landmark

Photograph: © Disney

10
Universal Orlando

www.universalorlando.com

29B2

1000 Universal Orlando Plaza, Orlando (I-4/Exit 74B or 75AB)

(407) 363 8000 or 1-800 232 7827

Daily from 9am; closing times vary

Both parks offer a choice of dining options, from snack stops and counter service cafés to full restaurants

Very good

Very expensive

Wet 'n' Wild (➤ 43)

Filming a New York street scene

Blockbuster rides, shows and attractions recreate movie magic and comic strip heroes at Universal's two Florida theme parks.

Disney may have greater worldwide recognition, but for many visitors to Orlando—particularly adult and teenage thrillseekers—Universal delivers a more exciting theme park experience. The original, movie-orientated, Universal Studios Florida theme park opened in 1990, sharing a site with the largest working movie and television production facility outside Hollywood. It soon developed a worldwide reputation for innovative, state-of-the-art thrill rides, such as the groundbreaking 21-million giga-watt Back To The Future... The Ride simulator experience. Recently the excellent and extremely popular Shrek 4-D and Revenge of the Mummy have added two brand new reasons to visit Universal.

In 1999, Universal Studios Florida metamorphosed into Universal Orlando, a complete resort destination with on-site hotels, the 30-acre (12-ha) CityWalk shopping, dining and entertainment complex, and a second theme park, Islands of Adventure. Adrenaline junkies are in for a treat at Islands of Adventure, which styles its roller-coaster and thrill rides after Marvel comic book heroes such as Spider-Man, Doctor Doom and the Incredible Hulk. A further range of entertaining rides and shows features the likes of Sinbad the Sailor, Jurassic Park's dinosaurs, children's favorites Dr Seuss and Popeye.

After dark, all the action moves to CityWalk, which boasts the world's biggest Hard Rock Café, attached to a 2,200-seat auditorium, a movie megaplex, shopping, nightclubs, jazz, and a wide variety of themed restaurants, ranging from a NASCAR Café for motorsports fans to a very laidback Key West-styled Jimmy Buffett's Margaritaville.

See also ➤ 38–43.

What To See

Above: *Gourmet food*
Right: *Busch Gardens*

27

Orlando

In the 1930s, traffic signals in downtown Orlando wore a sign admonishing drivers to be quiet. There were fresh fruit juice stands on the sidewalk and the city resembled "a great, cultivated park." Since Orlando has become synonymous with theme parks, it is generally assumed to be a loud, brash place.

Living in the shadow of the Mouse has certainly brought radical changes. The mini-Manhattan of the downtown district is bounded by highways, and the sky is busy with jets coming to and going from the international airport. But the city of Orlando has not succumbed entirely to the trappings of the tourist industry. There are pockets of greenery in Lake Eola and Harry P. Leu Gardens, and recent developments have included the renovated historic district around Downtown, the Orlando Science Center and its satellite art and history museums, and the palatial Orange County Convention Center.

> *"Orlando has been a favorite resort for a type of visitor ... [who] believes his health and longevity depend upon orange juice and the local brand of sunshine."*
>
> The WPA Guide to Florida
> (1939)

Orlando

Orlando's untidy outline sprawls either side of I-4, the fast interstate highway that slices diagonally across Central Florida from Tampa on the Gulf of Mexico to Daytona on the Atlantic Coast.

The city has extended steadily southwards towards Walt Disney World Resort and Kissimmee, and most visitors who stay in Orlando are based south of the city in the International Drive resort area. SeaWorld, Discovery Cove and Universal Orlando are just off I-Drive (as International Drive is familiarly called), which is served by the I-Ride bus.

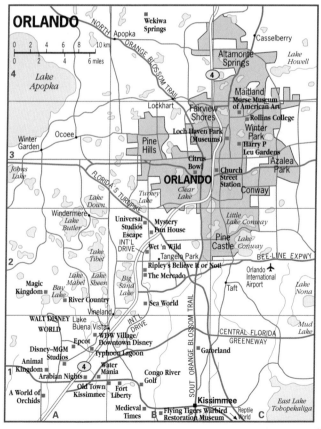

ORLANDO

NORTH ORANGE BLOSSOM TRAIL

0 2 4 6 8 10 km
0 2 4 6 miles

Wekiwa Springs

Apopka

Casselberry

Altamonte Springs

Lake Howell

Lake Apopka

Maitland
Morse Museum of American Art

Lockhart

Fairview Shores

Rollins College

Winter Garden

Ocoee

Pine Hills

Loch Haven Park (Museums)

Winter Park

Harry P Leu Gardens

Jobns Lake

Citrus Bowl

Church Street Station

Azalea Park

ORLANDO

Conway

FLORIDA'S TURNPIKE

Lake Down

Turkey Lake

Cléar Lake

Windermere
Lake Butler

Universal Studios Escape

Mystery Fun House

Little Lake Conway

INT'L DRIVE

Wet 'n Wild

Pine Castle

Lake Conway

Lake Tibet

Tangelo Park

BEE-LINE EXPWY

Ripley's Believe It or Not!

The Mercado

Orlando International Airport

Magic Kingdom

Lake Mabel Lake Sheen

Big Sand Lake

Taft

Lake Nona

Bay Lake

River Country

Sea World

Vineland

WALT DISNEY WORLD

Lake Buena Vista

INT'L DRIVE

Mud Lake

Epcot

WDW Village/ Downtown Disney

Disney–MGM Studios

Typhoon Lagoon

CENTRAL FLORIDA GREENEWAY

Gatorland

Animal Kingdom

Water Mania

Arabian Nights

Old Town

Congo River Golf

A World of Orchids

Kissimmee

Fort Liberty

Kissimmee

East Lake Tohopekaliga

Medieval Times

Flying Tigers Warbird Restoration Museum

Reptile World

SOUTH ORANGE BLOSSOM TRAIL

A   B   C

29

Opposite: *White sand beaches and tropical lagoons at Discovery Cove*

What to See in Orlando

It may come as a suprise to the vast majority of visitors who never venture beyond the distinctly touristy environs of I-Drive and the major theme parks, but Orlando does have more to offer than the well-traveled strip of hotels, motels, discount malls and smaller attractions that constitute the city's main resort area. This section deals with Orlando itself, while charming Winter Park, neighboring Kissimmee, and other attractions further afield are covered in Around Orlando ➤ 45–69.

DISCOVERY COVE ✪✪✪

A limited admission, by reservation-only, marine park adjacent to its big sister attraction SeaWorld (➤ 21, 36–7), Discovery Cove offers a whole day's worth of marine encounters as well as its dolphin-swim experience. Created on a far more intimate scale than the traditional Orlando mega-parks, Discovery Cove prides itself on the personal touch with impressive service levels including one member of staff to every eight guests.

The kid gloves treatment begins when you are greeted by a personal guide and taken on an orientation tour. For the dolphin-swim in one of the three large lagoons, small groups of six to eight (three to four groups per lagoon) and a trainer wade into shallow water to meet the dolphins and learn some of the hand signals the trainers use to communicate with their 30 or so Atlantic bottlenose charges. The group then moves into a deep-water lagoon for one-to-one swimming and playing with the friendly mammals—the experience, however, is surprisingly brief.

The marine thrills aren't over yet. Guests can snorkel amongst thousands of tropical reef fish from 90 different species in a coral reef setting, while sharks and barracudas patrol just a few inches away behind plexiglass safety panels. At Ray Lagoon wade into a world of sleek and mysterious rays as dozens of southern and cownose stingrays, which can grow up to 4ft (1.25m) across, glide past to be touched and fed little snacks. There is plenty of

www.discoverycove.com

⊕ 29B2
✉ 6000 Discovery Cove Way (I-4/Exit 71 or 72)
☎ (407) 370 1280 or 1-877 434 7268. reservations can also be made on-line
◷ Daily 9–5.30
🍽 Lunch in the Laguna Grill included; snack cabanas ($)
♿ Very good, includes wheelchairs adapted for sandy beaches
💲 Very expensive, minimum age for dolphin swim is 6; a reduced price package is available for cildren 3–5 and guests who do not take part in the dolphin swim
❓ While you'll have to make reservations well in advance, you can never predict the weather. If a storm closes the park, they'll try—if possible— to reschedule your visit to a convenient day

space to relax on the sandy beaches around the resort-style swimming pool. Some 5,000 tons of sand have been imported to lend that all important realistic feel to the scene with its beach chairs and colorful cabanas. Another option is to take a gentle meander down Tropical River. The river flows at a lazy 5–7mph (8–11kph) past sunken ruins and hidden grottoes, waterfalls and beaches to the 12,000-sq ft (1,115-sq m) aviary. This lushly landscaped free-flight enclosure, with its waterfall centerpiece, houses around 300 birds from the tiny finches and hummingbirds to substantial toucans and elegant demoiselle cranes. For an additional fee, you can get behind the scenes. The park offers a Trainer for a Day program for just 12 guests a day where you can work side-by-side with animal experts.

A day at Discovery Cove may seem like a very expensive option (about $250), but keep in mind that everything is included from towel and snorkel to wetsuit, and you'll have a very nice lunch that enhances your day.

31

GATORLAND ●●

Southeast of Orlando, on the border with Kissimmee, a pair of giant alligator jaws forms the entrance to this classic Florida attraction. Hundreds of captive "gators" occupy various pens and pools. There are alligator shows, alligator meals (try Gator Nuggets in Pearl's Smokehouse), and alligator products, such as wallets, boots and handbags, on sale in the gift shop. Other Gatorland residents include Florida crocodiles and caymans, native snapping and soft-shell turtles, and snake displays feature venomous rattlesnakes and cottonmouth moccasins.

A highlight is the 2,000-ft (610-m) long marshland boardwalk edging a cypress swamp. This is a native habitat alligator breeding ground and a great birdwatching spot. In spring, snowy egrets construct their nests within a few feet of passers-by, and there are great and little blue herons, pigeon-sized little green herons and dozens of other wading birds living in the water's edge rookeries.

HARRY P. LEU GARDENS ●●●

Sloping down to the shores of Lake Rowena, these lovely 50-acre (20-ha) gardens provide a soothing escape from the hustle and bustle. They were originally laid out by local businessman Harry P. Leu and his wife, who purchased the property in 1936 and lived in historic Leu House, a much-enlarged pioneer home in the middle of the gardens.

Near the entrance, the lush Ravine Garden leads down to a boardwalk and a gazebo which overlooks the lake. Coots and ducks potter about in the lake's waters and the occasional wild alligator lurks here. To the west of the property, mature southern magnolias and spreading live oaks shade the camellia woods, which can be seen at their

---

+ 29B1
✉ 14501 S Orange Blossom Trail
☎ (407) 855 5496 or 1-800 393 5297
◔ Daily 9am–dusk
🍴 Pearl's Smokehouse ($)
♿ Good
✋ Expensive

+ 29C3
✉ 1920 N Forest Avenue
☎ (407) 246 2620
◔ Daily 9–5 except Christmas Day. Leu House tours daily 10–3.30
♿ Good
✋ Moderate
↔ Orlando Museum of Art, Orlando Science Center (➤ 34–35)

best during the October to March flowering season. The Leus planted more than 2,000 camellia specimens here, and their collection is considered to be one of the finest in the eastern US.

The floral centerpiece is the Rose Garden, a popular setting for open-air weddings among the 1,000 scented rose bushes. Close by, Leu House is open for regular tours. In the far corner of the gardens, the Display Greenhouse is a riot of hothouse orchids, tropical gingers, anthuriums, heliconias and ferns.

Above: *One of Gatorland's scaly residents*
Left: *A giant pair of alligator jaws from the entrance to Gatorland*

HERITAGE SQUARE ✪

A focus for downtown Orlando, the Heritage Square development has been designed to symbolize "the heart of the community." This is the site where the city's early pioneers would have plotted out the land and planned its development. The old Orange County Courthouse is here, recently refurbished to house the Orange County Regional History Center (➤ 34), and the almost 2-acre (1-ha) park and plaza has been attractively landscaped with native trees, plants and Floridian-inspired landmarks as well as a pop-jet fountain that is a magnet for children.

🔳 29C3
✉ Central Boulevard at Magnolia Avenue (I-4 to exit 82C/Anderson Street)
↔ Orange County Regional History Center (➤ 34)

MENNELLO MUSEUM ✪

Florida's only folk art museum and a delightful find for fans of the genre. The workds of Earl Cunningham (1893–1977) form the basis of the collections courtesy of Florida collectors Michael and Marilyn Mennello, who are donating 44 of Cunningham's works to the museum over 13 years. Cunningham, who could list chicken farmer, seaman and junk dealer amongst his former careers, favored "historical-fantasy" themes and his colorful palette adapts superbly to exuberant depictions of typically Floridian scenes from florious Technicolor sunsets and native birdlife to Seminole villages and lively marine paintings featuring his favorite early 20th-century schooners. The museum also hosts regular visiting exhibitions of modern and antique paintings and sculpture.

✉ 900 E Princeton Street (I-4 to exit 85)
☎ (407) 246 4278
🕐 Tue–Sat 11–5, Sun 12–5. Closed Mon
♿ Good
✋ Inexpensive
↔ Harry P. Leu Gardens (above), Orlando Museum of Art (➤ 34), Orlando Science Center (➤ 35)

29C3
One Heritage Square, 65 E Central Boulevard (I-4 to Exit 82C/Anderson Street)
(407) 836 8500
Mon–Sat 10–5, Sun 12–5
Good
Moderate
Heritage Square (➤ 32)

ORANGE COUNTY REGIONAL HISTORY CENTER ✪✪

Unfortunately, many visitors—and quite a number of residents—believe Florida was discovered by Walt Disney. At this first-class museum, historians try to set the record straight by focusing on the people and society that existed in the pre-theme park years. In the handsomely restored 1927 Orange County Courthouse (➤ 32), the Center recalls Central Florida history through imaginative audio and visual presentations as well as hands-on exhibits. You are greeted by The Dome, a three- dimensional showcase for Florida icons, followed by an orientation experience. Suitably immersed in local lore, exhibits whisk you back in time to the Paleo-Indian era and a Timucuan village, the arrival of the Spanish explorers, a pioneer Cracker homestead, and the Roaring 20s when Tin Can tourists in Model-T Fords descended on Florida in their thousands.

Right: *Orlando Museum of Art has a renowned pre-Columbian collection*
Opposite: *Vincent van Gogh's Self-Portrait in Front of an Easel created from 10,000 picture postcards at Ripley's Believe It or Not!*

29C3
Loch Haven Park, E Princeton Street (I-4/Exit 85)
(407) 896 4231
Tue–Sat 10–5, Sun 12–5. Closed Mon
Good
Inexpensive
Harry P. Leu Gardens (➤ 33), Orlando Science Center (➤ 35)

ORLANDO MUSEUM OF ART ✪

The museum invites tourists to experience Orlando's cultural side and frequently hosts touring art shows, so check current schedules. If the permanent collections are on show, visitors will be rewarded with a notable collection of pre-Columbian art—some 250 pieces dating from around 1200BC to AD1500—plus works by leading 19th- to 20th-century American artists and African art exhibits.

ORLANDO SCIENCE CENTER ✪✪

Topped by a distinctive silver observatory dome, Orlando's impressive Science Center opened its doors in 1997. The exhibits are laid out over four levels and include dozens of interactive displays and hands-on educational games designed to appeal to children of all ages—and not a few adults as well.

On ground level, the NatureWorks Florida habitat section combines models and living exhibits such as turtles, baby alligators and a reef tank, and there is the excellent KidsTown early learning area for 8s and under. On Levels 2, 3 and 4, more elaborate and sophisticated exhibits tackle the basics of physics, mathematics, applied technologies and human biology in comprehensible and entertaining style. Movie moguls should definitely see the TechWorks exhibit on Level 4, which explores the behind-the-scenes tricks of the movie trade.

In addition, there are daily science-orientated shows in the Darden Adventure Theater and the Digistar Planetarium, and large format film presentations in the CineDome, which boasts a massive 8,000sq-ft (732sq-m) IMAX screen. On Friday and Saturday nights, while the CineDome features 3-D laser light shows, the Observatory welcomes stargazers.

RIPLEY'S BELIEVE IT ✪✪ OR NOT! ORLANDO ODDITORIUM

A whacky, lop-sided building tipping down an imaginary sinkhole, a hologram greeting from the long-dead Robert L. Ripley and hundreds of curious, eccentric and downright bizarre exhibits add up to a fairly unbelievable attraction. Robert Ripley was a connoisseur of oddities. Traveling extensively in the 1920s and 1930s, he amassed enough material to stock more than a dozen "museums" of this type worldwide. Typical exhibits include a Mona Lisa made from 1,426 squares of toast and a three-quarter scale model of a 1907 Rolls Royce Silver Ghost made out of 1,016,711 matchsticks and 63 pints of glue.

🗓 29C3
✉ 777 E Princeton Street (I-4/Exit 85)
☎ (407) 514 2000
🕐 Tue–Thu 9–5, Fri–Sat 9–9, Sun 12–5. Closed Mon, Thanksgiving and Christmas
🍴 OSC Cafe ($)
♿ Very good
💲 Moderate
↔ Harry P. Leu Gardens (► 33), Orlando Museum of Art (► 34)

🗓 29B2
✉ 8201 International Drive
☎ (407) 345 0501 or 1-800 998 4418
🕐 Daily 9am–1am
♿ Good
🚌 I-Ride, Lynx #42
💲 Moderate

35

➕ 29B2

✉ 7007 SeaWorld Drive,
Orlando (I-4/Exit 71 or72)

☎ (407) 351 3600

🕐 Daily 9–7 (extended
summer and hols)

🍴 Nine restaurants ranging
from cafeteria-style to full
service ($–$$$), plus
snack stops.
Reservations for Dine
With Shamu, Sharks
Underwater Grill and
Makahiki Luau should be
made in advance on
☎ 1-800 327 2424

🚌 I-Ride, Lynx #42

♿ Very good

🎟 Orlando FlexTickets offer
reduced rates and
flexibility. Available from
participating parks,
4-Park tickets provide
unlimited admission to
SeaWorld Orlando,
Universal Orlando and
Wet 'n' Wild. 5-Park
tickets include Busch
Gardens in Tampa

❓ Guided tours of Terrors of
the Deep, Wild Arctic
and the animal rescue
and research facility can
be made at the Guided
Tours counter near the
entrance. For Sharks
Deep Dive, the False
Killer Whale, Animal Care,
plus the guided
Adventure Express Tour
of the park, advance
reservations are
recommended, ☎ 1-800
432 1178 (press 5)

SEAWORLD ORLANDO ✪✪✪

SeaWorld's well-balanced combination of sights and shows is a proven winner. Unlike some parks, where the shows are incidental to the main action, here they are an intrinsic ingredient, and the rest of the attractions—plus behind-the-scenes tours (➤ panel)—can be fitted in as visitors make their way around the many and various show stadiums.

Unusual dining options in the park include Dine with Shamu and the classy Sharks Underwater Grill. Sunset reveals another side of SeaWorld, with nightly laser and fireworks displays and the **Makahiki Luau Dinner and Show**. Below is a list of highlights; see also ➤ 21.

Sea Lion and Otter Stadium Sea lions, otters and lumbering walruses are incorporated in the melodramatic swashbuckling tale, "Clyde and Seamore Take Pirate Island." Weaving cute tricks into the story highlights the animal attraction.

Journey to Atlantis Rickety Greek fishing boats transport guests on a sight-seeing trip to the newly risen City of Atlantis when disaster strikes and a high-speed water ride with special effects ensues.

Key West at Sea World A Florida Keys themed area, with a tropical atmosphere and street performers. The centerpiece is 2-acre (1-ha) Dolphin Cove, a lagoon habitat for Atlantic bottlenose dolphins adjacent to the Whale & Dolphin Stadium. Rescued turtles bask on the rocks of Turtle Point, visitors can feed and pet captive stingrays in the Stingray Lagoon, and there are nightly festivities in Sunset Square.

Kraken More thrills aboard a mega sea serpent-styled roller-coaster.

Manatees: The Last Generation? A distant aquatic relative of the elephant, the manatee is now a seriously endangered species. There may be fewer than 2,000 of these giant Florida sea cows left in the wild. All the manatees in this SeaWorld

exhibit are rescued and will be returned to the wild if possible.

Pacific Point Preserve California sea lions, harbor seals and South American fur seals occupy this rocky northern Pacific coast re-creation, complete with wave machine.

Penguin Encounter Some 200 enchanting Antarctic penguins and their Arctic cousins, the alcids (better known as puffins and mures), inhabit these icy confines.

Shamu Adventure An introduction to the world of the killer whale hosted by animal expert Jack Hanna. Makes a good preface to the Shamu stadium shows.

Shamu's Happy Harbor Play area for small children with climbing apparatus, radio-controlled boats, a sandpit and face-painting activities.

Terrors of the Deep Scene-setting, spooky music and eerie lighting accompany these aquariums full of lurking moray eels, 28-mph (45-kph) barracudas and highly toxic puffer fish. Ride the perspex tunnel through the 660,000-gal shark tank, or get really up close and personal with the park's daring interaction program, Sharks Deep Dive, and don a wesuit for a ride through the habitat in a shark cage.

Wild Arctic A simulated helicopter ride transports visitors to an Arctic base station for close encounters with polar bears, beluga whales and walruses. However, the icy habitats appear distinctly cramped for these large animals.

Below: *A fascinating underwater exhibit provides a clear view of all the drama and action of the sea*
Inset: *Killer whales on form at SeaWorld*

The famous Universal Studios globe symbol is a favorite photo backdrop

🕂 29B2

✉ 1000 Universal Plaza, Orlando (I-4/Exit 74B or 75AB)

☎ (407) 363 8000 or 1-888 322 5537

🕐 Daily from 9am; closing times vary

🍴 Both parks offer a choice of dining options from snack stops and counter service cafés to full service restaurants

♿ Very good

💰 Very expensive. Orlando FlexTickets offer reduced rates and flexibility. Available from participating parks, 4-Park tickets provide unlimited admission to SeaWorld Orlando, Universal Studios Escape and Wet 'n' Wild for 14 consecutive days. 5-Park tickets include Busch Gardens in Tampa. For further information ☎ 1-800 224 3838.

↔ Wet 'n' Wild (➤ 43)

UNIVERSAL ORLANDO

Ride though the movies at Universal Studios and escape to the fantasy world of legends and comic book heroes at Islands of Adventure. These two top theme parks are the twin poles of the Universal Orlando resort.

See also ➤ 26.

UNIVERSAL STUDIOS

It would be a mistake to assume that if you have done Walt Disney World Resort's Disney-MGM Studios (➤ 77–9) you should skip this. The Universal experience is more ride-orientated than its Disney rival and the attractive layout is a definite plus. The most popular shows on the Universal lot include the Beetlejuice's Graveyard Revue; Blues Brothers soul-style entertainment; and Animal Planet Live!, a spin-off of a popular US TV show showcasing talented animals. Below is a list of highlights.

Back to the Future…The Ride One of the most ambitious theme park rides ever created, this four-minute, spin in Doc Brown's time-traveling DeLorean is a must, with its wild simulator action and 70mm IMAX screens.

Earthquake: The Big One It is a short step off the San Francisco street set to this subway journey from hell. Experience an 8.3 on the Richter Scale, as portrayed in the classic 1974 disaster movie *Earthquake*.

ET Adventure A gentle ride over 3,340 miniature buildings aboard flying bicycles with ET in a basket on the front handlebars. A ride that appeals to younger children.

Jaws Set amid the seaside architecture and artfully arranged lobster pots of a re-created fishing village, Captain Jake's Amity Boat Tours embark for a wholly expected watery encounter with the glistening jaws of Universal's famous 32-ft (10-m), three-ton mechanical great white shark. The steel-and-fibreglass shark moves at speeds of up to 20ft (6m) per second, with a thrust power equal to a 727 jet engine. Passengers still love it, and this is a particularly attractive corner of the park.

Jimmy Neutron: Boy Genius A nickelodeon children's TV animated favorite, Jimmy has lept from small to large screen and now merits his very own theme park ride. Bucket along in the boy genius' Rocket Pod to rescue the world from evil egg-shaped Yokian aliens.

MEN IN BLACK Alien Attack An interactive chase through the streets of New York in hot pursuit of invading aliens. Terrific techno-futuristic styling, wild manoeuvres and weapons that rack up your score from hero to loser.

Nickelodeon Once the production center of the popular network, this is now a bare-bones attraction that allows parents to take their kids to a stage where a variety of games are played. The winning child has the honor of being creamed by a pie or getting drenched with slime.

Below: Face-to-face with Jaws

Bottom: The world's first life-size, ride-through video game—MEN IN BLACK Alien Attack

Revenge of the Mummy The horrors and highlights of the popular Brendan Fraser film are presented here, within the frightening passages and tombs of a darkened pyramid. Super scary effects and a roller coaster race in the dark have made this a highlight.

Shrek 4–D An adventure for the swamp-dwelling ogre and his lovely bride, Princess Fiona. Share the couple's honeymoon on 4-D "Ogrevision" complete with multi-sensory effects (including alarming pneumatic seats). The entertaining pre-show catches up non-fans on the storyline, and the show itself is a nice, fast-paced 3-D bridge between the original movie and its sequel.

Terminator 2: 3-D Battle Across Time The world's first 3-D virtual adventure, "T2:3-D"

Above: *No expense was spared creating the 3-D effects for T2:3-D*

(to aficionados) reunited the *Terminator 2* team to produce the most expensive film, frame for frame, ever made: $24 million for 12 minutes. The audience is transported into an apocalyptic world, showered with 3-D flying debris and whirlygig mini-hunter pocket gunships, and menaced by the flexi-steel pincers of the re-generating T-1,000,000. Fantastic effects: not to be missed, however long the line.

Twister... Ride It Out Lifted from the blockbuster movie, this multi-million dollar tornado encounter is not for the faint-hearted. Brave a five-story-high cyclone, complete with torrential rain and howling winds.

Universal Horror Make-Up Show After seeing props and make-up effects from classic horror films, you enter a theater where a host and a special effects expert deliver a side-splittingly fun and funny presentation on make-up and movie tricks.

Woody Woodpecker's KidZone A child-friendly zone of scaled down rides, adventure play areas and shows to delight the very young. Teeny thrills on Woody Woodpecker's Nuthouse Coaster, sing-a-long with the dinky dinosaurs in A Day In The Park With Barney, let off steam in Fievel's Playland or cool down amongst the water jets of the interactive Curious George Goes to Town play area.

Above: *Fun for youngsters on Woody Woodpecker's Nuthouse Coaster*

ISLANDS OF ADVENTURE

Universal employed the creative genius of movie director Steven Spielberg to help bring favorite comic strip characters and mythical legends to life in their second Florida theme park. Islands of Adventure claims to be the most technologically advanced theme park in the world

combining a host of hair-raising rides and boldly drawn, imaginative surroundings. Unlike its sister park, where the rides and attractions bear little relation to the stylized districts they inhabit, Islands of Adventure has five distinctively themed "islands" linked by footbridges and water transportation from the Port of Entry. The park's highlights are listed island by island below.

Jurassic Park A lushly landscaped "island" with a familiar theme based on Spielberg's blockbuster movie. Enjoy an overview of the district from the Pteranodon Flyers aerial runway; get up close and personal with an extraordinarily lifelike "animatronic" dinosaur at the Triceratops Encounter; and prepare to ride the Jurassic Park River Adventure past a further collection of cunningly constructed prehistoric creatures with a dramatic 85-ft (26-m) waterfall plunge as a finale.

Lost Continent A mythical world lost in the mists of time, the Lost Continent draws its inspiration from tales of Greek gods, Arthurian legend and the Arabian Nights. Dominating the skyline is Dueling Dragons, an intricately designed twin roller-coaster featuring a convincing near-miss scenario; young children are relegated to the scaled-down Flying Unicorn coaster nearby. There are action-packed thrills, stunts and towering pyrotechnic effects involved in The Eighth Voyage of Sindbad show, but the most elaborate attraction here is Poseidon's Fury: Escape From The Lost City entered via a swirling water vortex hurling 17,500gal (79,545L) of water around a 42-ft (13-m) tunnel. The subsequent battle between the water god and his archrival, Zeus, employs a further 35,000gal (159,091L) of water and flame effects.

Marvel Super Hero Island Universal's 21st-century technology has been used to create three state-of-the-art thrill rides in this primary-coloured, larger-than-life land fit for super heroes.

Above: Watch a Raptor hatch at the Jurassic Park Discovery Center

Below: The Incredible Hulk Coaster at Marvel Super Hero Island

Overhead, the giant green Incredible Hulk Coaster (it glows in the dark) blasts riders from 0 to 40 mph (65kph) in two seconds before embarking on a heartline inversion, seven roll-overs and two subterranean plunges. Across the street, guests are shot to the top of the twin 200-ft (61-m) steel towers of Doctor Doom's Fearfall before plummeting back down to earth. There is plenty of techno wizardry on display at the do-not-miss Amazing Adventures of Spider-Man, which combines moving ride vehicles, spooky 3-D action and special effects in a running battle with the forces of evil out to kidnap the Statue of Liberty; and there is more special effects action in the Storm Force show spectacular.

Seuss Landing From optimum thrills to the whimsical world of Dr. Seuss, this island is especially geared towards

smaller children. An assortment of suitably bizarre Seussian creatures serve as mounts on the Caro-Seuss-el, reputed to be the most elaborate carousel ever built. The One Fish Two Fish Red Fish Blue Fish ride invites guests to steer their own guppy through a series of water features guided by a special rhyme: lose the rhyme and get doused by a squirt post. If I Ran The Zoo is an interactive play area; while the best ride for accompanying adults is The Cat In The Hat, an entertaining journey through scenes from the classic story enlivened by special effects.

Toon Lagoon Betty Boop, Beetle Bailey and Hagar the Horrible leap out of two-dimensions and into outsize "life" on Comic Strip Lane, the main drag of Toon Lagoon. The lagoon in question is home to Me Ship, The Olive, a child-friendly play area aboard Popeye the Sailor's galleon. A short stroll away, Popeye & Bluto's Bilge-Rat Barges shoot the rapids in a whitewater raft ride that offers an ideal way to cool down on a hot day. And for a distinctly splashy flume ride, the first ever to send passengers below water level, sit tight for Dudley Do-Right's Ripsaw Falls.

Top left: The Cat in the Hat welcomes visitors to the If I Ran the Zoo play area

Bottom left: Wet 'n' Wild claims more rides than any other water park in Florida

WET 'N' WILD ✪✪

The hottest way to cool off on International Drive, this landmark water park offers dozens of thrills and spills, a scaled-down Kid's Park pool area and sunbathing decks. Top-rated heart-stopper is The Storm, a swirling body coaster with high speed chutes that lead into a wild whirl around a bowl and a splash landing. Other favorites include the 500-ft (152-m) twisting descent of the Black Hole, in total darkness; the seven-story Bomb Bay drop, and Der Stuka, one of the highest, fastest waterslides in the world. Family-sized inflatables tackle The Surge and Bubba Tub, or you can drift down Lazy River on a giant inner tube. See also ➤ 23.

🚩 29B2
✉ 6200 International Drive (I-4/Exit 75AB)
☎ (407) 351 1800 or 1-800 992–WILD
🕐 Daily 10–5 (extending from 9–9 in the summer); call for schedules
🍴 Concessions ($–$$)
🚌 I-Ride, Lynx #42
♿ Few
💲 Very expensive. Orlando FlexTickets offer reduced rates and flexibility. Available from participating parks, 4-Park tickets provide unlimited admission to SeaWorld Orlando, Universal Orlando (2) and Wet 'n' Wild over 14 consecutive days. 5-Park tickets include Busch Gardens in Tampa
🔁 Universal Orlando (➤ 26, 38–43)

Quality Inn

GREAT SERVICE

KEY W. K OLS

SEAFOOD · S EA

BREAKFAST

99

Around Orlando

An all-but-invisible line divides Greater Orlando from neighboring Kissimmee. Walt Disney World has transformed the former cattle town, bringing a welter of budget hotels and low-priced attractions along US192. Kissimmee is no beauty, but it is a useful family resort area, where the prices are fair, there are over 40,000 accommodations options and the entertainment is on tap.

Beyond Orlando and Kissimmee, Central Florida offers a wide choice of attractive day trips. Fast highways lead to top sightseeing destinations such as the Kennedy Space Center on the Atlantic coast and Tampa's Busch Gardens. Equally accessible are the horticultural highlights of Cypress Gardens and Bok Tower Gardens, and there are unspoilt state park preserves where hiking trails, canoe runs and wildlife-spotting provide the perfect antidote to the hurly-burly of the theme parks.

> *"Central Florida – a study in reality suspension, brought to your imagination by the nation's finest fantasy makers."*
>
> FLORIDA TOURIST BOARD

———————●———————

Left: *Larger-than-life signs line the street in Kissimmee*

*Colorful blooms at
A World of Orchids*

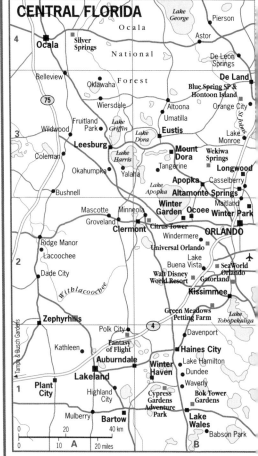

CENTRAL FLORIDA

[Map of Central Florida showing locations including:]

Lake George, Pierson, Ocala, Silver Springs, Astor, Ocala National Forest, Belleview, Oklawaha, De Leon Springs, De Land, Wiersdale, Blue Spring SP & Hontoon Island, Altoona, Orange City, 75, Fruitland Park, Umatilla, Wildwood, Lake Griffin, Lake Dora, Eustis, Lake Monroe, Leesburg, Coleman, Lake Harris, Mount Dora, Wekiwa Springs, Tangerine, Longwood, Okahumpka, Yalaha, Casselberry, Bushnell, Lake Apopka, Apopka, Altamonte Springs, Maitland, Mascotte, Minneola, Winter Garden, Ocoee, Winter Park, Groveland, Citrus Tower, ORLANDO, Clermont, Windermere, Ridge Manor, Universal Orlando, Lacoochee, Lake Buena Vista, SeaWorld Orlando, Dade City, Walt Disney World Resort, Gatorland, Withlacoochee, Kissimmee, Green Meadows Petting Farm, Lake Tohopekaliga, Zephyrhills, Polk City, 4, Davenport, Kathleen, Fantasy of Flight, Haines City, Auburndale, Winter Haven, Lake Hamilton, Plant City, Lakeland, Dundee, Highland City, Cypress Gardens Adventure Park, Waverly, Bok Tower Gardens, Mulberry, Bartow, Lake Wales, Babson Park, Tampa & Busch Gardens

0 20 40 km
0 10 A 20 miles
B

What to See Around Orlando

A WORLD OF ORCHIDS ✪

Harbored in a half-acre, climate-controlled greenhouse jungle, the world's largest permanent indoor display of flowering orchids is quite a sight. There are more than 2,000 orchid species on view and they come in an incredible array of colors, shapes, sizes and delicate scents, set against a lush backdrop of exuberant tropical foliage, gingers, palms and dramatic bird-of-paradise flowers. It is worth taking one of the daily guided tours (11 and 3; also 1 on weekends). Outside, native Floridian orchids can be seen from the short boardwalk nature trail; there is a catfish angling pool and exotic bird displays.

✚ 29A1
✉ 2501 Old Lake Wilson Road/CR545 (GM 5.5), Kissimmee
☎ (407) 396 1887
🕐 Tue–Sun 9.30–4.30. Closed New Year's Day, 4 July, 2nd and 3rd weeks in July, Thanksgiving, Christmas Day
♿ Few
✋ Free

46

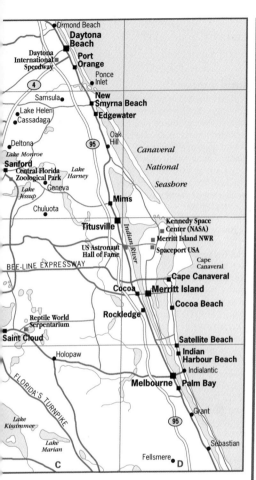

Elegant Bok Tower, on the Florida peninsula's highest point, Iron Mountain

BOK TOWER GARDENS ❂❂❂

Dutch philanthropist and publisher Edward W. Bok created these lovely woodland gardens in the 1920s and added the coquina rock and pink and gray marble bell tower, with its world-class carillon. Its 57 bronze bells range in weight from 17 to more than 22,000 lb (10,000kg) and toll each half hour. The tower is perched on top of Iron Mountain, the highest point on the Florida peninsula, at 298ft (91m) above sea level, and the gently sloping 157-acre (64-ha) gardens contain thousands of flowering azaleas, camellias and magnolias beneath a canopy of oaks, palms and pines. There are tours of the elegant 1930s Mediterranean Revival-style Pinewood House and Gardens in the grounds on certain days. A real haven for peace and serenity.

www.boktower.org
- 46B1
- ✉ CR17-A (off Alt. 27, 3 miles north of Lake Wales)
- ☎ (863) 676 1408
- 🕐 Daily 8–5
- 🍴 Garden Restaurant ($)
- ♿ Good
- 👜 Moderate
- ↔ Cypress Gardens (➤ 18, 52), Lake Wales (➤ 61)
- ❓ Daily carillon recitals at 3pm; concerts for special events.

www.buschgardens.com

46A1

Busch Boulevard, Tampa
(75 miles/121km west of
Orlando via I-4 West and
I-75 North to Fowler
Avenue/Exit 54)

(813) 987 5082 or 1-888
800 5447

Daily 10–6 (extended
summer and hols)

Refreshment stops
throughout park, plus:
Zagora Café (Morocco);
Das Festhaus (Timbuktu);
Crown Colony Restaurant
(Crown Colony); Vivi
Storehouse Restaurant
(Congo); Stanleyville
Smokehouse
(Stanleyville); Hospitality
House (Bird Gardens)
($–$$)

Very good

Very expensive.
Orlando FlexTickets offer
reduced rates and
flexibility. Available from
participating parks, 4-Park
tickets provide unlimited
admission to SeaWorld
Orlando, Universal
Orlando (2) and Wet 'n'
Wild over 14 consecutive
days. 5-Park tickets
include Busch Gardens in
Tampa. The park also
offers a range of behind-
the-scenes tours for an
additional charge. A guide
leads groups of up to 15
people on 4–5hr Guided
Adventure Tours; 30-
minute Serengeti safaris
allow closer contact with
the animals; and groups
of 7–10 participate in
feeding and training
encounters on Animal
Adventure tours

Check daily schedules for
show times

BUSCH GARDENS ✪✪✪

A popular side trip from Orlando, Busch Gardens provides a full day's family entertainment in a sprawling, African-inspired zoo-cum-theme park complex. The 10 themed areas each offer a choice of attractions and represents the perfect blend of animal shows, thrill rides and quiet nature walks. The fun water rides are very wet, and rainproof capes are on sale, but few sunbaked visitors bother. However, it is a good idea to bring a change of clothes to avoid a soggy journey back home. Opposite the Busch Gardens complex, Anheuser-Busch also have a popular 36-acre (15-ha) water park, Adventure Island (summer only).

Below is a list of highlights; see also ➤ 16.

Bird Gardens Flamingos, ducks, ibis and koi fish do battle with screeching gulls for titbits in the leafy lagoon areas of the Bird Gardens. There is a walk-through aviary, an eagle exhibit, bird shows and captive koala bears. On the edge of Bird Gardens, the duelling Gwazi roller-coaster rumbles over its 7,000ft (2,134m) of wooden track.

Congo An action-packed area at the northern extent of the park, the Congo's attractions include the hair-raising Kumba roller coaster. The slightly less dramatic Python still manages two 360° loops and a 70-ft (21-m) plunge. A drenching is guaranteed on the Congo River Rapids, and onlookers can man the Waterblasters on the bridge (25c a shot). The Ubanga-Banga Bumper Cars are located here, too; the Serengeti Express Railroad train stops at the station; and the park's magnificent Bengal tigers are incarcerated on undersized Claw Island.

Crown Colony Here you can eat at the park's only full-service dining room, the British Colonial-themed Crown Colony Restaurant. Look in on the Anheuser-Busch brewery's ceremonial draft horses and overlook the expansive Serengeti Plain as you dine on tasty entrees.

Egypt Ruined columns, giant carved figures and hieroglyphics provide the setting for a journey into Tut's Tomb, a walk-through tour of a replica pyramid tomb as discovered by the archaeologist Howard Carter in the 1920s. The contemporary news reel footage is fun, but the jewels look a little pasty. The big ride here is the 3,983-ft (2,214-m) long, 150-ft (46-m) high Montu roller coaster, featuring a heart-stopping inverted loop of 104ft (32m). The Serengeti Express Railroad train travels across the Serengeti Plain.

Land of the Dragons A well-designed adventure playground for small children, with a friendly dragon theme. The three-story Dragon's Nest treehouse is lavishly

Above: *The Tanganyika Tidal Wave*
Left: *Beyond Orlando, Busch Gardens is the most visited theme park in Florida*

equipped with stairs and ropeways, and there are slides, a sandpit, a carousel, watery activities and a children's theater. The Living Dragons display features monitor lizards, Komodo dragons from Indonesia and giant iguanas.

Morocco At the entrance to the park, Morocco features attractive Moorish-style architecture and a clutch of souk-like stores selling North African craft items. Ice shows are held at the Moroccan Palace Theater and other diversions scheduled in the Marrakesh Theater.

49

A close encounter with the wildlife at Busch Gardens

Serengeti Plain transport
🚋 Crown Colony. Sky Ride cable car: Crown Colony, Stanleyville. Serengeti Express Railroad: Egypt, Congo, Stanleyville

Nairobi First stop is Myombe Reserve: The Great Ape Domain, where the park's western lowland gorillas and chimpanzees nit-pick, snooze and occasionally stir themselves to get a better look at the humans. There are vampire bats, reptiles and snakes in Curiosity Caverns; baby birds and other residents in the Animal Nursery; a petting zoo, giant tortoises and elephants.

Serengeti Plain A 60-acre (24-ha) grassland enclosure reminiscent of the African veldt, inhabited by antelopes, giraffes, lions, rhinos and zebras. The park's Edge of Africa adventure promises a safari experience with close-up views of the animals, via a series of imaginatively designed enclosures, complete with a backing track of animal sounds and a range of evocative African smells running the olfactory gamut from camp fire to termite mound. Serengeti also boasts Rhino Rally, a rugged Land Rover Safari experience which packs thrills, spills and over 100 exotic African animals into it 8-minute journey.

Stanleyville Just the place to cool off with two great water rides: Tanganyika Tidal Wave (which soaks onlookers as well as passengers); and Stanley Falls Log Flume. There are reptile encounters at Snakes and More; the warthog and orangutan habitats; and a black spider monkey colony cavorting behind the fragrant and colorful Orchid Canyon. Guests can hop aboard the Serenget Express Railroad, shop for African crafts or enjoy family entertainments at the Stanleyville Theater.

Timbuktu At the heart of the park, Timbuktu's diversions include a semi-scary 3-D film at R. L. Stine's Haunted Lighthouse; all-singing, all-dancing perfomances at Das Festhaus; thrills aboard the Scorpion roller-coaster and other fairground attractions, plus arcade games.

A Tour Around Blue Spring State Park

One of the prettiest state parks in Central Florida, Blue Spring is also famous for its winter season manatee population. They usually visit between November and March, but the park is a great day out all year round, offering walking, boating and swimming opportunites, and it is a good place to enjoy a picnic.

From Orlando, take I–4 east (direction Daytona) to Exit 114. Follow US17–92 2.5 miles (4km) south to Orange City. Blue Spring State Park is signposted off to the right at the junction with W French Avenue.

A manatee breaking the surface of the water

Lying along the wooded banks of the St. Johns River, Florida's longest natural waterway, the park's namesake artesian spring is one of the largest in the US, producing around 100 million gallons (22 million liters) of water a day. It really is blue, too. The turquoise pool at the spring head is a popular swimming hole for snorkeling, scuba-diving or just splashing around to cool off in the heat of the day.

During winter the warm spring waters, which gush forth at a constant 72°F/22°C, attract manatees from the cooler waters of the St. Johns. From the waterside boardwalk there is a bird's-eye view of the manatees, and dozens of different fish and turtles swimming in the spring run; numerous waterbirds also congregate here. Canoes are available for rental and there are boat trips down the St. Johns to nearby Hontoon Island State Park.

Follow the walking trail which starts near the Steamboat-era Thursby House.

Thursby House itself is perched on top of an ancient shell mound, left by Timucuan Indians. The trail leads through sand pine scrub, marshland and flatwood areas of the park.

Return to Orange City and take US17–92/I–4 back to Orlando.

Distance
60-mile (97-km) round trip

Time
A 45-minute drive from Orlando. Allow at least 2 hours in the park

Start/end point
Orlando
✚ 46B2

Destination
Blue Spring State Park
✚ 46B3
✉ 2100 W French Avenue, Orange City
☎ (386) 775 3663
🕐 Daily 8am–sunset
💲 Inexpensive

Lunch
Snack concessions and cold drinks available in the park

51

➕ 47C3
✉ US17–92 (south of
1–4/Exit 52 towards
Sanford)
☎ (407) 323-4450
🕐 Daily 9-5, except
Thanksgiving and
Christmas
♿ Good
👐 Moderate

Below: *Southern belles,
in their antebellum
dresses, adorn the
grounds at Cypress
Gardens (➤ 53)*

➕ 29B1
✉ 4777 W Irlo Bronson
Highway/US192 (GM 12),
Kissimmee; also at 6312
International Drive,
Orlando
☎ (407) 396 6900
🕐 Daily 10am–late
♿ Few 👐 Moderate

CENTRAL FLORIDA ZOOLOGICAL PARK

In a way, the setting of the area's largest zoo distinguishes
it from others—it seems to be carved out from the Florida
wilderness. You'll exit the interstate highway to reach the
zoo, where shaded, winding boardwalks and paths take
you from exhibit to exhibit. The usual retinue of animals
are here pacing, hanging, strutting, and sleeping in what
you wish were larger or more natural enclosures. There
are elephants, cheetahs, mandrills and kookaburras and, in
the Herpetarium, an impressive line-up of venomous and
non-venomous snakes, lizards and frogs. Elsewhere, you'll
encounter pumas, llamas, sloths, monkeys, crocodiles and
alligators, turtles, iguanas and the beautiful bald eagle. The
zoo is about 20 miles (32km) northeast of downtown
Orlando in the city of Sanford.

CONGO RIVER GOLF & EXPLORATION CO ⭐

There is a choice of routes around this nifty mini-golf
course and players are challenged to follow in the
footsteps of 19th-century African explorers Henry Stanley
and Dr. David Livingstone. The obstacles are somewhat
less dramatic and debilitating than those encountered by
our heroes (there are no tsetse flies in Kissimmee), but the
tropical layout is well provided with waterfalls, streams and
mountainous boulders beneath the swaying palm trees.
For those "too pooped to putt," there are paddle boats
and a games arcade. At the second location on
International Drive, go-karts add to the fun.

CROSS CREEK ✪

This pleasant quiet rural community is home to the Majorie Kinnan Rawlings State Historic Site and well worth a visit if traveling brings you some 60 miles (97 km) to the north of Orlando. The author Majorie Kinnan Rawlings lived and worked in the tiny community for two years in the 1930s, where she bought a small homestead and settled down to learn about backwoods Cracker life. She immersed herself in the countryside, learning about every plant, shrub, tree and flower. She cooked on a wood-burning stove and washed her clothes in an iron pot. Neighbours soon warmed to her friendliness and her books reflect an intimate insight into the people and the locality. Her most famous novella was *The Yearling*, for which she won a Pulizter Prize.

You can visit the house, preserved just as she left it, complete with ancient typewriter on the porch.

✚ Off map to north

Marjorie Kinnan Rawlings State Historic Site

✉ Cross Creek (21 miles/34km southeast of Gainesville on CR 325)

☎ (352) 466 3672

🕐 Daily 9–5

🎟 Tours inexpensive

Congo River Golf

CYPRESS GARDENS ADVENTURE PARK ✪✪✪

Probably Florida's most sedate theme park, and its oldest, Cypress Gardens has until recently rather rested on its laurels, or rather its huge and colorful floral displays. The Botanical Gardens are still a treat with tropical plants on show such as heliconias, bromelaids, bougainvillea and bamboo, and there are impressive shows of massed blooms in the formal gardens, too. A recent addition of amusement rides has made it more popular for children.

Families enjoy a visit to the Wings of Wonder butterfly conservatory, where it is good fun to spot the hidden iguanas, turtles and tiny Asian doves. Birds of prey and reptile discovery shows are part of the Nature's Way animal habitat exhibit; and daily entertainment programs feature concerts, shows and water-skiing spectaculars on the lake.

See also ▶ 17.

✚ 46B1

✉ State Road 540 W, 4 miles (6.5km) east of Winter Haven (off US27, 22 miles (35km) south of I-4)

☎ (863) 324 2111

🕐 Daily 10–6 (extended for special events)

A Tour Around Mount Dora

Distance
60-mile (97-km) round trip

Time
A 50-minute drive from Orlando. Allow half a day to look around Mount Dora

Start/end point
Orlando
➕ 46B2

Destination
Mount Dora
➕ 46B3

Lunch
Windsor Rose English Tea Room ($)
✉ 142 W 4th Avenue
☎ (352) 735 2551

A pretty lakeshore town set amid gently rolling countryside and citrus groves, Mount Dora is renowned for its Victorian architecture and antiques shops.

From Orlando, take the Orange Blossom Trail/US441 north (direction Ocala) to Mount Dora, and follow signs for downtown.

Northern settlers first arrived on the shores of Lake Dora in the 1870s, and built their town on a low rise overlooking the eastern end of lake. The oldest surviving building in town is the 1883 Lakeside Inn, 100 Alexander Street, a short step away from the Chamber of Commerce.

At the Chamber of Commerce, 341 Alexander Street (☎ (352) 383 2165), pick up a driving map indicating a 3-mile (5-km) route around the pick of Mount Dora's historic homes.

The attractively restored downtown district is fun to explore within the Historic Shopping Village; many of the old buildings house art galleries, specialty gift stores, tempting gourmet food emporiums and popular antiques shops. Also in downtown is Mount Dora's most impressive historic home, the splendid Queen Anne-style Donnelly House. Ornately decorated with ironwork, a cupola, copious gables, balustrades, balconies and yards of gingerbread trim, it now serves as probably the daintiest Masonic Hall in the land. Nearby, the town's former fire station and jail houses the small Royellou Museum, displaying local history exhibits. By the lake

Donnelly House, a Queen Anne-style confection in downtown Mount Dora

there is a nature trail in Palm Island Park; boats and bicycles are available to rent. It's a touch of New England in the heart of Florida.

Return to Orlando on the US441 or SR46/I–4.

FANTASY OF FLIGHT ✪✪✪

Aviation historian, aerobatic pilot, designer and vintage aircraft restorer Kermit Weeks' museum showcases exhibits from Weeks' private aircraft collection alongside history displays and entertaining simulator rides.

Aviation buffs will find plenty to enjoy here down among the World War I fighters, 1920s barnstormers, Spitfires, Wildcats and Dauntless dive bombers from World War II—and even a battered Japanese Zero fighter, rescued from the treetops of New Guinea in the early 1990s. Aviation oddities are featured too, such as the Roadair flying automobile with retractable wings for highway driving, and an accurate replica of Charles A Lindbergh's *Spirit of St. Louis*, which made the first trans-atlantic flight in 1927. You can take a tour behind the scenes to see restoration workshops.

See also ► 19.

🔲 46A1
✉ SR-559, Polk City (I-4 West to Exit 44)
☎ (863) 984 3500
🕐 Daily 9–5

GREEN MEADOWS PETTING FARM ✪✪

A great treat for small children, who can find the theme park experience and crowds a bit overwhelming. Here they can scamper about safely, clamber on tractors, collect acorns for the pigs and encounter all manner of other farmyard animals on the two-hour tours that allow them to meet and touch calves, lambs, kids, turkeys and fluffy yellow ducklings. Every child can milk a cow (if he or she wants to), and enjoy waggon rides and pony rides.

Free-ranging guineafowl, peacocks and chickens peck and preen around the attractive tree-shaded compound, which provides good protection from the hot sun, and toddlers or babies can be towed around in miniature farm trailers. Picnickers are welcome.

www.greenmeadowsfarm.com
🔲 46B2
✉ 1368 S Poinciana Boulevard, Kissimmee
☎ (407) 846 0770
🕐 Daily 9.30–5.30 (last tour 4pm)
🍴 Snacks, sandwiches and cold drinks available ($)
♿ Few 💰 Expensive

Above: *Green Meadows Petting Farm, a gentle alternative to alligators*

Food & Drink

Orlando knows a bit about mass catering. From sunrise to sunset and long into the night, the city's 4,300-plus restaurants, cafeterias, family diners and take-away operations aim to satisfy the hunger of a wildly divergent public, and on the whole they do pretty well.

Breakfast

For most visitors planning a long, busy day out and about sightseeing, the day begins with a traditional American breakfast, selected from a menu as long as your arm. Stockpile energy in the form of cereals, hot waffles or pancakes, served with bacon and maple syrup, eggs and hash browns, sweet fruit or bran muffins, toast or plain "English muffins." In general, hotel buffet breakfasts are reasonably priced, and several motels and suite hotels include a basic breakfast of cereal, muffins and pastries with coffee and fruit juice in the room price.

A typical American breakfast

Florida Specialties

Florida's two main food groups are commonly known as "surf 'n' turf"—that's seafood and beef. There are dozens of seafood restaurants in Orlando serving fresh fish, crab, lobster, shrimp and other delicacies. Steak houses and barbecue restaurants also do a roaring trade, and there is plenty of Southern-style Cajun or Creole influence in dishes, such as tasty blackened chicken or fish coated in spices and cooked over the grill.

Lunch

Lunch on the sightseeing trail often means alarming lines in the theme parks. The busiest time is between 12 and 2, so if you can manage to eat earlier or later it does make things easier. Guests who prefer a sit-down meal in a service restaurant at lunchtime should make reservations at the Guest Relations window when they arrive at the park. Otherwise there is usually a wide choice of eateries, from self-service cafeterias to hot dog stands, barbecue take-aways, sandwiches, burgers and ice creams, which can be eaten at outdoor seating areas.

Dinner

The evening meal is a very flexible affair in Orlando. Some restaurants start serving at 4pm to cater for those who have missed out on lunch or determined budget eaters who make the best of "early bird specials," discounted meals offered before the restaurants really begin to fill up at around 6.30–7.

The main non-Walt Disney World Resort areas—

International Drive and Kissimmee—are well provided with inexpensive family restaurants and fast food chains, as well as medium-price range steak houses, American, Chinese, Italian and Mexican eateries. For something more up-market, look to the top hotels, such as the Peabody Orlando, for a chance to dress up and enjoy a gourmet meal in notably elegant surroundings.

Above: Traditional ribs

Below: Delicious, freshly squeezed fruit juice — essential on a hot day

Medium-price bracket and expensive hotels generally provide a choice of dining options, and this is certainly true of the Walt Disney World Resort complexes. Restaurants serving up a selection of walking, talking oversized Disney characters along with their menu are a favorite with children, but do remember to reserve ahead to avoid disappointment (➤ 97 panel).

Drinking

Sightseeing is thirsty work in Orlando, and several rounds of soft drinks for the whole family at theme park or hotel prices can prove an expensive business. If you are on a budget, it is a good idea to stock up on bottled water, fruit juices or multi-packs of canned soft drinks at a supermarket. To buy or consume alcohol legally in the state of Florida, customers must be 21 or over.

Tip
To reduce the cost of drinks, when at the theme parks, buy the souvenir glass that can be refilled free of charge throughout the day.

A Tour Around Merritt Island National Wildlife Refuge

Distance
100-mile (161-km) round trip; 120 miles (194km) as part of a day trip including Kennedy Space Center

Time
A 1¼ hour drive from Orlando; allow 40 minutes for the Black Point Wildlife Drive

Start/end point
Orlando
✚ 46B2

Destination
Merritt Island National Wildlife Refuge ☎ (321) 861 0667)
✚ 47D2

Lunch
Take a picnic or eat at the Kennedy Space Center—restaurants, cafés, snack concessions ($–$$)

To see what Florida looked like before any development, take a drive to the Merritt Island National Wildlife Refuge. It was protected mainly due to the variety of birds and animals that call it home, but also to prevent anyone from encroaching on the adjacent land the government had claimed for the Kennedy Space Center. The refuge occupies 220sq miles (564sq km) of marshland wilderness harboring some 300 species of birds and dozens of other types of wildlife.

Take the Bee Line Expressway/SR528 toll road east from Orlando to SR407 north. Follow signs for the Kennedy Space Center onto SR405. At US1, turn left (north) and go through Titusville. At the junction with SR406, turn right, cross the Indian River, and continue to the Black Point Wildlife Drive on the left, and follow this for 7 miles (11km).

The northern portion of Merritt Island is a rare natural habitat preserve spanning fresh- and salt-water lagoons, mangrove islands, oak hardwood hammocks and palmetto-covered sand dunes, providing breeding grounds for an enormous variety of native Floridian wildlife. Endangered species such as manatees, wood storks and bald eagles live here, and sea turtles come ashore to lay their eggs on the Canaveral National Seashore in summer. At Stop 1, a viewfinder points out bald eagles' nests; at Stop 5, hundreds of wading birds can be seen feeding

This nature conservation area's habitats range from pocket-sized freshwater lagoons to vast saltwater estuaries

on the mud flats at low tide; and the 5-mile (8-km) Cruickshank Trail, a circular walk from Stop 8, has an observation tower a few minutes' walk from the parking area.

Return on SR406, then turn right on SR402 for the Visitor Center.

The Center provides more information about the Refuge, and a further choice of walking trails.

KENNEDY SPACE CENTER ✪✪✪

The Kennedy Space Center offers a unique opportunity for the public to learn about the people and machines behind the US space program. A visit comprises a number of elements, including narrated bus tours of the historic Cape Canaveral Air Station facility and the unmissable Kennedy Space Center tour, which includes a photo stop in clear sight of the landmark Launch Complex 39, and the giant Vehicle Assembly Building, where the shuttles and their possible successors are prepared. Visitors can stop off as long as they like at the state-of-the-art Apollo/Saturn V Center with its excellent Apollo 8 launch experience, and a complete 363-ft (11-m) long Saturn V rocket on display.

At the main Visitor Complex, IMAX theaters present space themed programs, of which the earth-shaking launch close-up *The Dream is Alive* is the best. Earthlings can wander around towering exhibits in the Rocket Garden, a collection of upright unlaunched rockets, clamber aboard a full-size shuttle replica and view objects such as space suits and astronaut food. You can catch a live show, but best of all attend Astronaut Encounter; every day a real astronaut takes the stage to talk about space travel and answer questions.

See also ➤ 20.

🛈 47D2
✉ SR405, Merritt Island (Bee Line Expressway/SR528 toll road east from Orlando to SR407 north, and follow signs)
☎ (321) 449 444 or (321) 454 4198 TDD
🕐 Daily 9–dusk
💲 Expensive
❓ Check schedules for the occasional Cape Canaveral: Then and Now tours

Historic spacecraft in the Rocket Garden

Did you know ?

French science fiction writer Jules Verne predicted Florida's space age future almost a century before NASA arrived on the scene. In his novel From Earth to the Moon, *published in 1863, Verne described 'Florida…shaken to its very depths' by the blast-off of a rocket called* Columbiad, *a name strangely similar to the Columbia orbiter launched in 1981.*

➕ 46B2

Silver Spurs Rodeo
☎ For information call (407)
677 6336

Kissimmee Sports Arena
✉ 958 S Hoagland
Boulevard
☎ (407) 933 0020
🕐 Fri 8pm–10pm

Old Town Kissimmee
✉ 5770 W Irlo Bronson
Memorial
Highway/US192 (GM
9.5), Kissimmee
☎ (407) 396 4888 or 1-800
843 4202
🕐 10am–11pm
🍴 Fast food, snacks, several
restaurants ($–$$)
♿ Few
🆓 Free
↔ Water Mania (► 66)

Above: *Kissimmee, a
popular vacation base
south of Orlando, and a
few minutes from Walt
Disney World Resort*

KISSIMMEE ✪

Kissimmee is an attractive location for budget travelers. This is the place to find reasonably priced accommodations close to Walt Disney World Resort, and most hotels offer a free shuttle to the Disney parks. Inexpensive family restaurants are the order of the day along US192, and there are supermarkets for self-catering holidaymakers and plenty of family attractions close by. To help visitors find their way around US192, the city has erected a number of Guide-Markers (GM) along the highway. These are used in this guide to locate the various attractions.

Kissimmee's main drag stretches for miles along the US192 east–west cross route, either side of I-4. Its seamless run of local attractions and small shopping centers, chain restaurants and low-rise hotels has been newly landscaped and made more visitor-friendly with sidewalks and pedestrian access, transportation links and even bicycle racks. The quiet downtown district, at the junction with Orange Blossom Trail, has now been restored.

A recreated turn-of-the-century Main Street, the **Old Town Kissimmee** open-air mall, provides an entertaining mixture of shops and half-a-dozen fairground rides, including the landmark Ferris wheel on the south side of Irlo Bronson Memorial Highway/US192. On Fridays and Saturdays a classic car parade takes place here in the evening.

One of the top rodeo events on the professional Rodeo Cowboys Association southeastern circuit, the **Silver Spurs Rodeo**, takes place at Kissimmee biennially in February and October, and weekly demonstrations of calf-roping, bareback riding, steer wrestling and other skills take place at the **Kissimmee Sports Arena** on Fridays.

See also Water Mania (► 66).

LAKE TOHOPEKALIGA ⭐⭐

A short step from downtown Kissimmee, Lake Toho (as it is commonly known) offers an idyllic escape from the crowds. The 13-mile (21-km) long lake covers around 22,700 acres (9,190ha), with several islands in the middle where Seminole Indians once built forts. The bass fishing is excellent, and there is great birdwatching, with more than 120 species of birds living around the lake or visiting—like the winter population of white freshwater pelicans, who fly 2,000 miles (3,225km) south to escape the chilly northern temperatures.

The 30-ft (9-m) *Eagle Ray* excursion boat takes passengers out on the lake from Big Toho Marina. Call **Aquatic Wonders Boat Tours** in advance and arrange for a half-day bass fishing trip with a knowledgeable guide, or a two-hour nature safari with a chance to see bald eagles, osprey, snail kites and more.

➕ 46B2

Aquatic Wonders Boat Tours
✉ 101 Lakeshore Boulevard
☎ (407) 846 2814
🕐 Daily 9–6 by reservation
💰 Expensive

LAKE WALES ⭐

If you'd like to experience Florida before amusement parks cropped up, visit Lake Wales. In a quiet section in the center of the state, there are still groves of oranges, grapefruit and tangerines, plus pristine lakes and Arts and Crafts cottages—and a palpable feeling of old Florida.

The **Lake Wales Museum and Cultural Center**, housed in a former railroad depot on the main street, features local history displays and railroad memorabilia. The other local attraction is Spook Hill, more correctly known as North Wales Drive. Visitors who drive to the bottom of the hill and put their vehicle in neutral at the white line will find that they appear to roll uphill.

➕ 46B1

Lake Wales Museum and Cultural Center
✉ 325 S Scenic Highway (Alt 27), Lake Wales
☎ (863) 678 4209
🕐 Mon–Fri 9–5, Sat 10–4
♿ Few
💰 Inexpensive
🔁 Bok Tower Gardens (▶ 47)

A beautiful Carolina wood duck, one of the many birds enjoying the waters of Lake Tohopekaliga

A Tour Around Ocala National Forest

Distance
95-mile (153-km) round trip

Time
1¼ hour drive from Orlando.
Spend the full day in the
Forest, or also plan to visit
Silver Springs (➤ 22, 63)

Start/end point
Orlando
✚ 46B2

Destination
Ocala National Forest
✚ 46A4

Lunch
Take a picnic, or there are
snack concessions at
Recreation Areas within the
Forest ($)

Within the boundaries of this 366,000-acre (148,178-ha) woodland preserve, the world's largest sand pine forest rolls back from the banks of the St. Johns River, sprinkled with nearly 1,000 lakes and criss-crossed by miles of walking trails, state parks, campgrounds and natural springs. Hikers will find peace and quiet along the numerous woodland paths. Other popular pastimes include paddling one of the beautiful canoe trails and fishing on Lake Dorr.

Take the Orange Blossom Trail/US441 north from Orlando to the SR19 exit at Eustis. Follow SR19 north for 11 miles (18km) to the Visitor Center at Lake Dorr; the main Ocala National Forest Visitor Center is on SR40, 12 miles (19km) east of Ocala.

Stop off at the Visitor Center for a free map and browse among the leaflets giving information about hiking trails and short walks. The Center can also supply details of fishing, canoeing and boating locations scattered around the forest. Ocala National Forest is at the heart of Central Florida's Big Scrub country, one of the few places Florida black bears still inhabit. It is also an important native habitat preserve for deer, wild turkeys, eagles and owls. Wading birds live here too, easily spotted from boardwalk trails.

Lakes in the National Park are popular for fishing and canoeing

Head for Juniper Springs Recreation Area at the head of the 7-mile (11-km) Juniper Creek canoe run.

This is a favorite spot, where canoe reservations can be made in advance (☎ (352) 625 2808). Other recreation areas, such as Alexander Spring and Lake Dorr, offer swimming, picnicking and boat rental.

Return to Orlando along the SR40, SR19 and US441.

REPTILE WORLD SERPENTARIUM ✪

Rather off the beaten track, east of St. Cloud, this no-frills serpentarium's main mission is research, and the collection and distribution of snake venoms. There are cobra and viper venom-gathering programs twice a day (at 12 and 3), and meticulous notes cover each snake display. Discover the secrets of the rattlesnake's tail, learn how to distinguish the non-venomous scarlet king snake from the poisonous eastern coral snake (same black, red and yellow coloring in subtly different proportions), and contemplate the world's largest snake species, the reticulated python and the massive green anaconda, known to snack on crocodiles in its native South America.

🔢 46C2
✉ 5705 E Irlo Bronson Memorial Highway/US192, 4 miles east of St Cloud
☎ (407) 892 6905
🕐 Tue–Sun 9–5.30. Closed Mon, Thanksgiving and Christmas
♿ Few
💲 Inexpensive

SILVER SPRINGS ✪✪✪

A Central Florida sightseeing destination since the 1870s, Silver Springs has augmented its natural attractions with a host of rides, shows and other essential modern-day theme park ingredients.

Alongside the ever-popular boat trips and jeep rides, favorite shows include the Alligator and Crocodile Encounter, which showcases 13 species of crocodilians and a rare white alligator, and Reptiles of the World, starring one of the alligator's few natural enemies, a 110lb (45kg) snapping turtle.

Swimming is permitted in the spring only during July, but for hot summer days the **Wild Waters** water park is conveniently located next door.

See also ➤ 22.

www.silversprings.com
🔢 46A4
✉ SR40, 1 mile (1.61km) east of Ocala (72 miles/ 116km northwest of Orlando)
☎ (352) 236 2121 or 1-800 234 7458
🕐 Daily 9–5.30 (extended summer and hols)
🍴 The Deli ($); Springside Pizzeria ($); Springside Restaurant ($–$$); Swampy's Smokehouse Buffet ($–$$); snack stops, ice creams and cold drinks stalls ($)
♿ Good
💲 Very expensive; no extra charge for concerts
↔ Ocala National Forest (➤ 62)

Wild Waters
✉ Adjacent to Silver Springs on SR40
☎ (352) 236 2121 or 1-800 234 7458
🕐 Mar–end Oct daily 10–7 (extended in summer)
💲 Expensive

A Silver Springs resident: A passing racoon gives a friendly wave

A Tour Around Wekiwa Springs State Park & Wekiwa River

Distance
36-mile (58-km) round trip to
Wekiwa Springs

Time
Orlando to Wekiwa Springs:
30 minutes

Start/end point
Orlando
 46B2

Destination
Wekiwa Springs State Park
 46B3
✉ 1800 Wekiwa Circle,
Apopka
☎ (407) 884 2008
🕐 Daily 8–sunset
💵 Inexpensive

Lunch
Take a picnic; snacks and cold
drinks are available in the park

The Wekiwa River is one of Central florida's prettiest natural waterways. An unspoilt tributary of the St. Johns, it flows on a lazy 15-mile (24-km) journey north and east before emptying into the main river near Sanford. The river borders the western edge of Seminole County, in an area known as the Central Florida Everglades. Just 344sq miles (882sq km) in total, Seminole County can boast some 2,000 freshwater lakes and rivers and offers numerous outdoor activities including walking, birdwatching, fishing and messing about in boats from gentle backwater canoe trips to airboat rides on alligator-infested Lake Jesup. The Wekiwa's headwaters rise in Wekiwa Springs State park.

Take I–4 eastbound from Orlando to Exit 94.
Head west on SR434, and look for the right
turn on to Wekiwa Springs Road, which leads
straight to the park.

This is a lovely woodland park with plenty of shade and over 13 miles (21km) of hiking trails. The main loop trail visits native habitat areas ranging from dry sand ridges to low, swampy areas close to the Rock Springs Run (be prepared for mosquitoes in summer); there are several shorter trails as well. Swimming is permitted in the refreshing main spring ("Wekiwa" means "spring of water" in Creek Indian), and canoes are available for rental

just beyond the wooden bridge crossing the main spring. Try it—a canoe trip will offer a vision of Florida few visitors take the time to see. You'll be going with the flow, paddling along a crystal clear stream as you drift beneath the shade of huge oak and cypress trees. If you want, you can paddle over to an adjoining stream to reach the Rock Springs Run.

Take I–4 back to
Orlando.

SPRINGS, CENTRAL FLORIDA ☆

One of the pure pleasures of Central Florida is lazing in the clear, cool waters of its natural springs. This is one of the few places in America where you can do this since a high limestone cap traps crystal clear 72°F (22°C) water just below the surface. The springs—most of which are safely protected within the boundaries of state parks—are just right for swimming, splashing, sunning, and paddling. In DeLand, there's great swimming and cuddly manatees at Blue Springs (➤ 13, 51), and a few miles north at DeLeon Springs are the ruins of an old sugar mill and a great swimming hole. In addition to Longwood's Wekiwa Springs (➤ 64), Alexander Springs and Salt Springs in the Ocala National Forest are two more tranquil swimming pools and each is surrounded by great hiking trails and woodlands. Information on admission prices, directions, and hours are posted at www.dep.state.fl.us/parks.

www.dep.state.fl.us/parks

US ASTRONAUT HALL OF FAME ☆☆

Recently amalgamated with the neighboring Kennedy Space Center, this is a popular stop with children, who enjoy the hands-on approach. There's lots of interactive fun here, along with space hardware exhibits from the Mercury and Gemini programs and entertaining rides such as Shuttle to Tomorrow, a flight into the future aboard a full-scale mock-up of a 120-ft (37-m) orbiter. Potential astronauts get to put themselves to the test with the G-Force Trainer, and another favorite attraction is the stomach-churning 3D–360° flight simulator ride—which is pretty good fun to watch as well. Many of the exhibits and objects were donated by the astronauts from their personal collections.

✚ 47D2
✉ 6225 Vectorspace Boulevard/SR405, Titusville
☎ (321) 269 6100
🕐 Daily 9–5 (extended summer and hols)
🍴 Cosmic Cafe ($)
♿ Good 🚻 Moderate
↔ Kennedy Space Center (➤ 20, 59), Merritt Island Wildlife Refuge (➤ 58)

An astronauts' showcase

WATER MANIA

This is the place to cool off in the height of summer or just enjoy a family day out. The 36-acre (15-ha) site features wave pools, lagoons, small children's watery fun areas and lazy inner tube rides on Cruisin' Creek. Thrill-seekers can shoot the body-surfing-style Wipe Out ride, the Screamer, the Double Berzerker, Twin Tornados, the blacked-out Abyss and curvaceous Anaconda. On a drier note, there are arcade games, mini-golf, beach volleyball and basketball, and picnic facilities.

WINTER PARK

A smart northern suburb of Orlando, Winter Park boasts a brace of fine art museums, an attractive shopping district and scenic boat trips on a chain of small lakes edged by millionaires' mansions. The town was originally laid out as a genteel winter resort for wealthy New Englanders in the 1880s. Its main street, Park Avenue, is lined with boutiques and art galleries, shops selling exclusive interior design knick-knacks and chic restaurants. On Saturdays, the local Farmers' Market, on New England Avenue, is a favorite stop for fruit and vegetable shopping and fresh-baked goods, or just browsing among the colorful stalls.

Morse Museum of American Art Pride of place goes to the gallery's world-famous collection of Tiffany glass, much of it salvaged from Laurelton Hall, Louis Comfort Tiffany's Long Island home, which burned down in 1957. Many of Tiffany's own favorite pieces are on display, such as the glorious Rose Window. There are earthy fruit and vegetable stained-glass still lifes, others depicting magnolia blooms and elegant wisteria lampshades. Further collections cover ceramics, furniture and metalwork, and Tiffany's contemporaries also get a look in, with glassware from René Lalique and Emile Galle, paintings by Maxfield Parrish, and contributions from Frank Lloyd Wright.

Rollins College and Cornell Fine Arts Museum At the southern end of Park Avenue is the delightful campus of Florida's oldest college. Established in 1885, Rollins' original campus buildings were constructed in fashionable Spanish-Mediterranean style on a pretty campus overlooking Lake Virginia. Near the entrance to the campus, the Walk of Fame features more than 400 stepping stones gathered from the birthplaces and homes of famous people, from Mary, Queen of Scots and Benjamin Franklin to Buffalo Bill. There is an attractive college chapel and theater linked by a loggia, and the Cornell Fine Arts Museum houses notable collections of European Old Master paintings, 19th- and 20th-century American art, Indian objects and decorative arts.

Opposite: *Splashtacular fun at Water Mania*

Cornell Fine Arts Museum
- ✉ Rollins College, Holt Avenue, Winter Park
- ☎ (407) 646 2526
- 🕐 Tue–Fri 10–5, Sat–Sun 1–5. Closed Mon
- ♿ Good
- 🎫 Free

Outstanding works of art can be found at the Cornell

Scenic Boat Tours A chain of six little freshwater lakes around Winter Park is linked by narrow, leafy canals. The canals were once used to transport logs, but now facilitate the movement of small boats and allow scenic boat trips to putter from Lake Osceola down to Lake Virginia and up to Lake Maitland. The tours last about an hour and offer a prime view of Winter Park's most exclusive lake frontage—the grandest homes overlook Lake Maitland. Waterbirds are easy to spot and there is the occasional glimpse of an alligator.

Scenic Boat Tours
- ✉ 312 E Morse Boulevard, Winter Park
- ☎ (407) 644 4056
- 🕐 Daily 10–4 on the hour, except Christmas
- ♿ Few
- 🎫 Moderate

In the Know

If you only have a short time to visit Orlando, or would like to get a flavor of the region, here are some ideas:

10
Ways To Be A Local

Dress comfortably and coolly. Floridians are also casual dressers and jackets and ties for men are rarely required.
Game on Check out Orlando's action-packed sporting scene from Orlando Magic's basketball skills to baseball spring training (➤ 112).
Gator wrestling is best left to the professionals. Instead, watch a demonstration at Gatorland (➤ 32).
Go fishing—this is how the locals relax, leaving the theme parks to visitors.
"Have a nice day" is not just an automatic platitude in Orlando: people really mean it.
Sample grits, the breakfast porridge of the Southern US, made from roughly ground boiled corn mixed with butter.
Tipping is a way of life here, not just in bars and restaurants, but for just about any kind of service from valet parking to shuttle bus drivers.
Tolls are payable on the Bee Line Expressway and Florida Turnpike, so keep some small change accessible in the car.
Turn right on red at traffic lights in Florida unless a stop sign dictates otherwise—but look out for other road-users and pedestrians.
Western wear is high fashion during Kissimmee's famous rodeo events. Snap up a pair of alligator-skin boots (➤ 107).

10
Good Places To Cool Off

Blizzard Beach (➤ 88).
Blue Spring (➤ 51).
Canaveral National Seashore offers miles of unspoilt seashore and beaches north of the Kennedy Space Center.
Cocoa Beach is one of Florida's famous "party" beaches on the Atlantic Coast, an hour's drive down the Bee Line Expressway/SR528.
Central Florida Springs (➤ 65).
Tanganyika Tidal Wave at Busch Gardens (➤ 50).
Typhoon Lagoon (➤ 90).
Water Mania (➤ 66).
Wekiwa Springs (➤ 64).
Wet 'n' Wild (➤ 23, 43).

10
Best Theme Park Restaurants

To make advance reservations, contact Guest Relations on entering the park.
Makahiki Luau
✉ SeaWorld Orlando
☎ (407) 363 2559.
Dinner-only South Seas feast and entertainment (call ahead to make

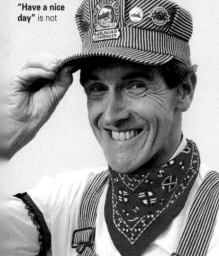

reservations).

Brown Derby ✉ Disney-MGM Studios, Walt Disney World ☎ (407) 939 3463. Cool and clubby replica of Hollywood moguls' meeting place. Pasta, steaks, Cobb salad.

Chefs de France ✉ Epcot, Walt Disney World ☎ (407) 939 3463. Elegant Disney outpost for French *nouvelle cuisine*.

Coral Reef ✉ Epcot, Walt Disney World ☎ (407) 939 3463. First-class seafood and a stunning view of the coral reef exhibition.

Crown Colony ✉ Busch Gardens, Tampa ☎ (813) 987 5600. Family restaurant overlooking the animals of the Serengeti Plain exhibit. Chicken dinners, fresh seafood, sandwiches.

Emeril's Orlando ✉ Universal CityWalk ☎ (407) 224-2424. Chef Emeril Lagasse's upscale and elegant restaurant serving such delights as pan-seared grouper, sauteed shrimp and baked Maine lobster.

Hard Rock Café ✉ Universal Studios, CityWalk, Orlando ☎ (407) 351 7625. Big fun, big name rock memorabilia and big burgers.

Liberty Tree Tavern ✉ Magic Kingdom, Walt Disney World ☎ (407) 939 3463. All-American home-style cooking in a re-created colonial inn. Turkey dinners, Cape Cod pasta, pot roast.

Lombard's Landing ✉ Universal Studios Florida, Orlando ☎ (407) 224 6401. Seafood specialties, pasta and steaks, plus waterfront dining in the re-created San Francisco district.

Sharks Underwater Grill

✉ SeaWorld Orlando ☎ (407) 351 3600. Fresh fish and Floribbean cuisine.

10 Top Golf Courses

Arnold Palmer Golf Academy ✉ 9000 Bay Hill Boulevard, Orlando ☎ (407) 876 5362.

Black Bear Golf Club ✉ 24505 Calusa Boulevard, Eustis ☎ (352) 357 4732 or 1-800 423 2718.

Celebration Golf Club ✉ 701 Golf Park Drive, Celebration ☎ (407) 566 4653.

Disney's 99 Holes of Golf ✉ Walt Disney World Resort, Lake Buena Vista ☎ (407) 824 4321.

Faldo Golf Institute by Marriott ✉ 12001 Avenida Verde, Orlando ☎ (407) 238 7677

Grand Cypress ✉ Grand Cypress Resort, North Jacaranda, Orlando ☎ (407) 239 1904.

MetroWest Golf Club ✉ 2100 S Hiawassee Road, Orlando ☎ (407) 299 1099.

Orange County National Golf Center ✉ 16301 Phil Ritson Way, Winter Garden ☎ (407) 656 2626 or 1-888 PAR 3672

Stoneybrook Golf Club ✉ 2900 Northampton Avenue, Orlando ☎ (407) 384 6888.

Timacuan Golf & Country Club ✉ 550 Timacuan Boulevard, Lake Mary ☎ (407) 321 0010.

10 Free Attractions

Audubon's Center for Birds of Prey ✉ 1101 Audubon Way, Maitland ☎ (407) 644 0190. Aviaries housing birds of

prey, including eagles, owls and hawks.

Bradlee-McIntyre House ✉ 130 W Warren Avenue (at CR427), Longwood ☎ (407) 332 0225. Orange County's only Victorian cottage.

Cornell Fine Arts Museum ✉ Rollins College, Winter Park ☎ (407) 646 2526. Exhibitions of old masters and contemporary fine arts (▶ 67).

Fort Christmas Park ✉ 1300 Fort Christmas Road, Christmas ☎ (407) 568 4149. Replica fort, pioneer homes and Seminole War exhibits.

Lake Eola Park ✉ Eola Drive, Orlando ☎ (407) 246 2827. Downtown's lakeside park with picnicking areas, children's playground and boat rentals.

Kraft Azalea Gardens ✉ Alabama Drive, Winter Park. Azaleas, subtropical plants and cypress trees on shore of Lake Maitland.

Lakeridge Winery & Vineyards ✉ 19239 N US27, Clermont ☎ (352) 394 8627 or 1-800 768 9463. Guided tours and tastings.

Maitland Historical Museum & Telephone Museum ✉ 221 W Packwood Avenue, Maitland ☎ (407) 644 2451. Artifacts, photos and memorabilia.

West Orange Trail ✉ Winter Garden ☎ (407) 877 0600. A 4.5-mile (7km) trail for walkers, cyclists and skaters (bicycle and skate rental available).

Zora Neale Hurston National Museum of Fine Arts ✉ 227 E Kennedy Boulevard, Eatonville ☎ (407) 647 3307. Exhibits by artists of African descent in Zora Neale Hurston's (▶ 14) home town.

Walt Disney World Resort

Walt Disney World Resort is the apogee of the Disney phenomenon. It is a fairytale fiefdom, where litter and spoilsports are banned and Cinderella Castle pops out of the storybook and into 3-D reality. Disney's appeal is universal. It makes nonsense of age and cultural barriers uniting people from all walks of life in the pursuit of good, clean family fun and escapist fantasy. Teams of "imagineers" have resurrected everybody's favorite characters, then added the latest screen stars, state-of-the-art rides, shows and even gently educational exhibits spread over the theme parks, water parks and entertainment districts.

Some find it all too perfect, and Disney's reputation for ruthless efficiency leads to charges of blandness. However, the prime objective here is family entertainment and that, even the most grudging cynic has to admit, Disney delivers in abundance.

> *"I have never called this art. It's show business, and I am a showman."*
>
> WALTER ELIAS DISNEY,
> (1901–66)

———————•———————

Left: *Fun on Big Thunder Mountain Railroad*

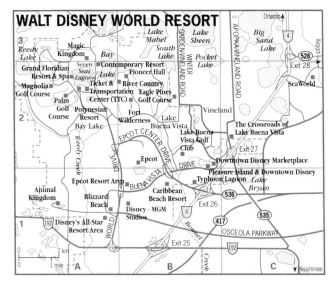

WALT DISNEY WORLD RESORT

🔲 29A1 (and above)

✉ Walt Disney World
Resort, Lake Buena Vista
(I-4/Exits 25-B and 26-B,
south of Orlando)

☎ (407) 824 4321

🕐 Check current schedules

🍴 Each park offers a wide
choice of dining options
open for breakfast, lunch,
dinner, and snacks
throughout the day.
Priority seating (bookings
service at Guest
Relations) is advised for
table service restaurants
($$–$$$)

🚌 Free shuttle bus services
from many Orlando/
Kissimmee hotels

♿ Excellent

💵 Very expensive. Note that
children of 10 and over
qualify for adult tickets;
children's tickets are for
ages 3–9; under 3 free

Walt Disney World Resort

The cooler winter months are the most comfortable time to visit Walt Disney World Resort, and the crowds are definitely less pressing either side of the Christmas rush (January until mid-February, and mid-September until Christmas, with the exception of the busy Thanksgiving holiday). However, expect to stand in line whenever you go, and be well prepared with loose, comfy clothing, sturdy footwear and sunblock.

Ticket options: Daily One Park/One Day admission tickets are valid for one park only on the stated day but if you plan to stay for several days, which you should do, multiple-day "Magic Your Way" base tickets offer flexibility and savings. The multi-day passes are good for one park each day your ticket is valid. For an additional $35, you can add the "park hopper" option to a ticket and have the privilege of racing from one park to the next. Another add-on is the Magic Plus Pack, which will cover admission to Disney's water parks, Pleasure Island, or the DisneyQuest video arcade. It is best to do your homework before you arrive and check online for ticket configurations. Keep in mind that unused days never expire and can be used on a future visit. Guests at certain properties can purchase the **Ultimate Park Hopper**, which provides admission to all Disney's WDW attractions.

   FASTPASS Save time standing in line for the most popular rides in all four Disney theme parks with the

FASTPASS system. Simply pop your regular park ticket into the FASTPASS machine at the attractions offering the complimentary service and you will receive a designated return time with no need to wait. The FASTPASS allows a one-hour window from the time printed on the ticket during which you should present yourself at the FASTPASS entrance with your ticket and sail straight through. You can only have one FASTPASS running at any one time, i.e. you must have used (or exceeded the time allocation for) one FASTPASS before you can collect another. Attractions offering this service are indicated on Disney maps and in this guide by the letters (FP).

What to Expect The Disney parks provide a wide range of guest facilities, from baby strollers and lockers to banking and kenneling. A limited number of wheelchairs are available, and there are special arrangements for sight- and hearing-impaired visitors. Guest relations can also help with lost and found queries, camera rentals and free battery-charging.

? Details of daily parades, showtimes and night-time fireworks and laser displays are printed in current park guides. Hotel, campground, show and ticket reservations can be made through Central Reservations (☎ 407/934 7639, fax (407) 354 1866). Dining reservations can be made up to 60 days in advance (☎ (407) 939 3463).

Main Street, U.S.A. in Magic Kingdom Park, leading up to Cinderella Castle

Photograph: © Disney

72A1

Osceola Parkway, Walt
Disney World Resort

(407) 824 4321

Check current schedules

Fascinating Facts
If you washed and dried one
load of laundry every day for
44 years, you would clean as
much as the Walt Disney
World Resort Laundry handles
in a single day.

Around 450,000 miles
(725,806km) of lawn are
mown at Walt Disney World
Resort each year: the
equivalent of 18 trips around
the equator.

Enough Mouse Ear hats are
sold every year to cover the
head of every man, woman
and child in Pittsburgh.

*Come face to face with
zebras and giraffes*

DISNEY'S ANIMAL KINGDOM

Walt Disney World Resort's fourth full-scale theme park,
Disney's Animal Kingdom, focuses Disney's famous imagination and attention to detail on the natural world. The
500-acre (202-ha) site features five themed districts and
has more than 200 animal species showcased in re-
created naturalistic habitats. Not content with the wonders
of the world about us, Disney has also gone for the
populist angle with DinoLand U.S.A., a fun celebration of
the dinosaur era. Amongst all the fun and games,
however, care has been taken to incorporate a worthy
conservationist message.

For the best chance of seeing the animals at their most
active, it pays off to arrive at Disney's Animal Kingdom as
early as possible in the day. From The Oasis entry point,
head for Safari Village and the footbridge links to the other
four districts. Then secure your first FASTPASS (▶ 72).

Africa & Rafiki's Plant Watch African-styled Harambe
Village is the start point for two excellent big game viewing
opportunities. Kilimanjaro Safaris (FP) is Disney's Animal
Kingdom's unmissable ride, a Jeep journey deep into the
re-created African veldt inhabited by lions, cheetahs,

Photograph: © Disney

Did you know ?

More than 4 million plants, including 100,000 trees and 4 million grasses and new shrubs, were used to create the exotic and varied landscapes of Disney's Animal Kingdom, and there are more than 350 types of grass growing here. On a less realistic note, The Tree of Life has 103,000 hand-painted leaves.

More Fascinating Facts

Walt Disney World Resort has a daily population of 200,000 people.

More than 2,600 couples get married at Walt Disney World Resort every year.

If all the hot dogs and hamburgers consumed by Walt Disney World Resort guests each year were lined up end to end they would stretch from Orlando to Philadelphia.

Walt Disney World Resort generates 70 tons of waste every day, of which 35 tons is recycled on site.

rhinos, giraffes, wildebeest, zebras and others. The ride is brought to a rather abrupt end by a rescue mission to save the elephants from poachers, but the Pangani Forest Exploration Trail allows a closer look at some of the safari animals, notably an underwater view of the hippos, plus a lush and misty gorilla habitat. Mosey on down to Harambe Station to catch the Wildlife Express miniature train ride, which wends its way past the "backlot" animal quarters to Rafiki's Plant Watch. Here exhibits on endangered species are presented alongside picture windows viewing into the animal nursery and veterinary suite.

Asia Exuberant rainforest-type foliage and colorful tropical flowers set the tone for the Maharaja Jungle Trek, a gentle stroll through elaborate Indian temple ruins to the tiger enclosure and exotic bird aviaries. After the trek, visit the Flights of Wonder birds of prey show, or down a cool drink in the leafy Siamang Viewing Area. Asia's action adventure is the Kali River Rapids (FP), a whitewater rafting ride that shoots beneath tunnels of overhanging bamboo, past giant boulders and cooling water jets. A new roller coaster ride, Expedition Everest!, creates cutting edge excitement as it rushes forwards, backwards, up and down as you try to steer clear of the Abominable Snowman.

Camp Minnie-Mickey Set slightly from the main bustle, this is a good place for families with young children to take a break. Camp Minnie-Mickey's character greeting areas field a full team of classic Disney figures. Pocahontas and Her Forest Friends is a cute child-oriented show with live animal performers; while the Festival of the Lion King is a real crowd-pleasing spectacular for all ages, featuring acrobatic routines, fire-jugglers and stilt-walkers. And check schedules for Mickey's Jammin' Jungle Parade, which tootles through the camp every afternoon.

DinoLand U.S.A. Prehistory with a Disneyesque spin begins at the Olden Gate Bridge, a 40-ft (12-m) Brachiosaurus skeleton marking the entrance to DinoLand U.S.A. First stop for kids is The Boneyard play area. Follow this with a visit to the Fossil Preparation Lab, where real life paleontologists undertake their research into dinosaur remains, while guests are dwarfed by the impressive collection of life-size casts taken from dinosaur skeletons in the Dinosaur Jubilee exhibition area. On the thrills front, there is rollercoaster action aboard Primeval Whirl! and the Dinosaur (FP) ride is a must, offering a time travel expedition back to the end of the dinosaur era. Dodge meteorite showers and ravening, blood-thirsty "animatronic" dinosaurs in an attempt to bring back a dear little veggie dino for posterity. For light relief, check out the Tarzan Rocks! acrobatic rock music extravaganza or take a four-person dino vehicle for a gentle "dino soar" with TriceraTop Spin.

Safari Village At the heart of Safari Village, The Tree of Life is the centerpiece and symbol of the park. The trunk, branches and root system of the 145-ft (44-m) tall landmark have been carved with 325 animal images and around its vast bulk the Safari Village Trails meander past assorted enclosures for lemurs, kangaroos, capybaras and other small- to medium-sized animals. Beneath the roots, a subterranean theater presents It's Tough to be a Bug (FP), an entertaining and imaginative 3-D look at life from a bug's perspective starring Flik and Hopper from *A Bug's Life*. (Some surprise effects could upset children scared of creepy-crawlies.)

DISNEY-MGM STUDIOS ✪✪

Disney-MGM Studios was Walt Disney World Resort's riposte to the news that Universal Studios was opening a rival theme park-cum-studio facility at Orlando in 1990. Disney squeezed in just ahead, opening in 1989, and have almost doubled the size of the original park, though it remains rather shorter on rides than its chief rival. However, there is

✚ 72B1
✉ Walt Disney World Resort
☎ (407) 824 4321

plenty of Disney flair on display and constantly updated exhibits showcase popular new productions, and give a chance to watch Disney's skilled animators at work.

Backlot Tour After a visit to the splash tank and a chance to participate in a demonstration of special effects at sea, hop aboard a tram to cruise past the Star's Parking Lot, the world's largest working wardrobe department, and the props and special effects departments. There are a couple of surprises in store at Catastrophe Canyon before arriving at the American Film Institute Showcase for a display of prize props and film memorabilia.

The Great Movie Ride On Hollywood Boulevard a full-scale re-creation of Mann's Chinese Theater is the setting for this ambitious homage to movie classics. Audio-Animatronics® figures replace the great stars in famous screen scenes.

Honey, I Shrunk the Kids Movie Set An imaginative children's adventure play area featuring giant bugs, spider's web rope ladders, looming blades of grass and cooling water jets for welcome relief on a hot day.

Photograph: © Disney

DinoLand U.S.A.

Transport across WDW

WDW Resort buses (free to WDW Resort guests and multi-day pass holders) service the parks from the main Transportation and Ticket Center at Magic Kingdom; journeys take up to 90 mins

The sprawling WDW site is difficult to negotiate, although the complex road system is well-signposted. There are considerable distances between the various parks and resort hotels, which make a car useful, though not essential.

Thrills on the Rock 'n' Roller Coaster Starring Aerosmith

Indiana Jones® Epic Stunt Spectacular! (FP) Check schedules with the updated show times listed in the park's free giveaway map, and catch a performance of this explosive stunt show. "Audience volunteers" get an opportunity to join in the fun.

Jim Henson's Muppet Vision 3-D (FP) Jim Henson's magnificent Muppets steal the show hands down. A terrific combination of big screen 70mm, 3-D film action, monster special effects and anarchic humor.

The Magic of Disney Animation A brief but illuminating insight into the world of animation that traces the long and painstaking road from a story idea to the finished product. Check out the original artworks in the animation gallery before the tour leads off through the production studios, where artists crouch over their drawing boards.

Rock 'n' Roller Coaster Starring Aerosmith (FP) A giant red electric guitar fronts this thrilling roller-coaster ride in the dark. After joining the heavy rock band Aerosmith at a studio session guests are invited on a limo race against time to reach the band's evening gig accompanied by a thumping soundtrack and some pretty hairy manoeuvres.

Sounds Dangerous Starring Drew Carey Seriously funny

man Drew Carey takes the lead in a spoof pilot for a new TV investigative show, *Undercover Live*, and explores the world of sound in a darkened theater. Most of the action takes place in a total blackout as the audience's ears are assailed by a trip to the

Did you know ?

The liftshaft drop in the Tower of Terror, Walt Disney World Resort's tallest attraction, is the equivalent of falling off the ears of the park's Earffel Tower. It takes just three seconds.

barber and a swarm of killer bees amongst other weird and wonderful soundsational experiences.

Star Tours A bone-shaking intergalatic thrill ride on a runaway space ship. Wild simulator action, dazzling special effects. The pre-flight warnings aimed at pregnant women, heart condition sufferers and the faint-hearted should also deter anybody who has eaten recently.

Theater of the Stars In a setting reminiscent of the Hollywood Bowl, the 1,500-seat Theater of the Stars hosts Beauty and the Beast Live—a cute mini-musical that kids love. The Hollywood Hills Amphitheatre is the setting for Fantasmic!—and evening extravaganza featuring fireworks, action songs and a salute to Disney film and music classics. It is hugely popular so arrive early for a good seat.

The Twilight Zone Tower of Terror™ (FP) A quiet stroll down Sunset Boulevard is soon interrupted by the shrieks of terrified passengers plummeting down the lift shaft of the spooky Hollywood Tower Hotel. Guests encounter various mysterious manifestations on the route to the top of the 199-ft (61-m) building before a series of plunges. Don't miss it.

Voyage of The Little Mermaid (FP) Beloved of little girls the world over, Ariel (The Little Mermaid of the title) gets the full theme park treatment as her story is retold with clever special effects, puppets, Audio-Animatronics, film clips and live performers.

Walt Disney—One Man's Dream Compiled as part of Disney's 100 Years of Magic Celebration!, this look at the theme park visionary's life and achievements features objects and previously unseen film footage.

Who Wants To Be A Millionaire—Play It! (FP) A chance for fans of the hit TV quiz to get a taste of the real thing in a meticulously recreated studio setting. Sadly no one actually wins a million, but there are prizes.

 72B2

✉ Epcot Center Drive, Walt Disney World Resort

☎ (407) 824 4321

🕐 Check current schedules

Epcot's trademark—the silver Spaceship Earth geosphere—is a time machine in which you ride from the past to the stars

EPCOT ✪✪

Walt Disney's original plan to create a Utopian-style research community living on the Epcot (Experimental Prototype Community of Tomorrow) site never came to fruition, but his ideas have been adapted to provide a semi-educational showcase for new technology and sciences and a window on the world around us.

Epcot, twice the size of Magic Kingdom, and twice as tough to navigate on foot, is divided into two parts. In the shadow of a giant silver geosphere, the Future World pavilions house the scientific stuff, with displays focusing on transport, communications, health, energy, agriculture and oceanology. This sounds rather serious, but the Walt Disney Imagineers have added plenty of hands-on fun,

Photograph: © Disney

rides and film shows. The second section of the park is World Showcase, a 1.3-mile (2-km) promenade through 11 "villages," each representing the potted history, culture and architecture of a different nation.

FUTURE WORLD

Innoventions Tomorrow's technology today, as top companies preview the latest developments in science and technology in an interactive environment. The two Innoventions pavilions are packed with hands-on fun from virtual tag games with Mickey and Minnie to video challenges designed to test players' problem-solving skills and knowledge of a range of science, technology and environmental subjects. Guests can build a family homepage at the Web Site Construction Zone, check out the future of the automobile, and tour the "smarthome" of tomorrow, which includes a robot dog amongst its innovations.

Journey into Imagination with Figment A lackluster presentation narrated by Monty Python stalwart Eric Idle, who shares the billing with a perky little dragon called Figment. The rides grinds through a series of colorful scenes purporting to represent an exploration of human imagination and deposits bemused passengers into the interactive ImageWorks area to experiment with their own images. Much more fun is the hugely entertaining Honey, I Shrunk the Audience (FP) 3-D show in the movie theater.

The Land There are three deservedly popular attractions here, starting with Living with the Land (FP). This gentle boat ride journeys through various environments explaining how plants survive, then continues into a futuristic greenhouse world where some of the fresh produce served in Walt Disney World Resort restaurants is grown. This is quite a sight as you glide past citrus trees laden with giant 9-lb (4-kg) lemons (each capable of producing two pints of juice) and string gardens where cucumbers, eggplants and banks of lettuces grow vertically. Guests who would like a closer look at The Land's experimental greenhouses should sign up for **Behind The Seeds**, a behind-the-scenes guided walk tour.

On the upper level of the pavilion, the Circle of Life Theater presents an excellent eco-conscious film show starring characters from *The Lion King*: Simba the Lion King turns Simba-the-Educator and talks Pumbaa and Timon out of polluting Africa with the Hakuna Matata Electric Disco Holiday Resort. Pretty hard-hitting stuff for Orlando.

New for 2005 is "Soarin." Sitting under the wings of a hang glider, you're hoisted 40ft (12m) high inside a giant projection screen dome, then you take off on a virtual aerial tour of California.

The Living Seas This 6-million-gallon salt water marine exhibit with an amazing man-made coral reef is inhabited by 2,000 colorful and curious tropical fish. An introductory

Recommended Epcot Restaurants

🍴 Future World: Coral Reef, The Living Seas
World Showcase: Chefs de France, France; L'Originale Alfredo di Roma, Italy; Nine Dragons, China; Mitsukoshi Teppan Yaki Dining Room, Japan

❓ Make lunch or dinner reservations at Guest Relations on entering park

Behind The Seeds

✉ Reservations at Green Thumb gift store, The Land pavilion

🕐 Tours (1 hour) depart every hour 10.30–4.40

💲 Moderate additional charge

A boat glides by the fabulous Morocco Pavilion

Photograph: © Disney

film prefaces the descent to Seabase Alpha for a ride through the aquarium to the observation levels for views of sharks, bottlenose dolphins and sea turtles. Manatees, Florida's endangered prehistoric sea cows, also feature.

Mission: Space A high-tech, high thrill ride that simulates a space adventure, which launches you from a pulse-racing, adrenaline-injected lift-off to a rendezvous with weightlessness and a rough landing on Mars. Hypercool.

Spaceship Earth A ride through the history of communications within the focal point of the park—a 180-ft (55-m) high aluminium geosphere. Dioramas illustrate man's progress from cave paintings to a neon journey down the Information Superhighway. Then passengers disembark into the AT&T Global Neighborhood and its diverting assortment of hands-on games with a futuristic flavor.

Test Track (FP) The longest and fastest ride ever created by Walt Disney Imagineers features road test automobile action. Take to the track for a tyre-squealing, three-story ascent and assorted high-speed manoeuvres in the dark.

Universe of Energy Ellen Degeneres stars with Bill Nye, the Science Guy, in a multi-screen—and occasionally humorous—presentation of the history and uses of

energy. A long pre-show is just the beginning. The entire presentation lasts 45 minutes, which is a lot of valuable vacation time spent watching fake dinosaurs and hearing about an oil giant's take on fossil fuels.

WORLD SHOWCASE

The American Adventure The centerpiece of the World Showcase villages presents a 30-minute dramatized history of America by Audio-Animatronic American icons Mark Twain and Benjamin Franklin.

Canada Feast the eyes on the CircleVision 360° *O Canada!* film and stock up on maple leaf motifs at a Rockies-style exhibit.

China A beautiful 360° film of Chinese people and provinces, museum-quality displays of historic objects from Imperial China and fabulously elaborate architecture.

France Recreated Belle Epoque Paris in the shadow of a miniature Eiffel Tower. Café dining, wine-tasting, waterfront artists and a French perfumerie.

Germany Storybook architecture with geranium-filled window boxes, plus traditional "oompah" music piped out over the popular *biergarten*.

Italy Venice's St. Mark's Square and the Doge's Palace recreated with immaculate scaled-down precision, including ice creams, arias and a notable restaurant.

Japan Wind chimes, temple drums and a pagoda, set beside manicured gardens and koi fish ponds, give an authentic twist to this shopping and dining complex.

Mexico A huge model of a pre-Columbian pyramid and a boat ride down the River of Time attract plenty of visitors to the colorful Mexican village.

Morocco An attractive Moorish souk set in narrow alleys and elegant tiled courtyards. Authentic belly-dancing displays in the restaurant.

Norway Malevolent trolls summon up a North Sea storm to rock the good ship *Maelstrom* (FP), a Viking longboat thrill ride in this popular Scandinavian village.

United Kingdom—or, rather, Merrie England: a jolly knees-up with Cockney pearly kings and queens in the Rose & Crown Pub, fish and chips, warm beer and street entertainers massacring Shakespeare.

Shop the World
The World Showcase villages offer unusual shopping opportunities. In Morocco's souk, genuine North African leatherwear, carpets, brass items and fezes make interesting souvenirs. Canada offers Indian and Eskimo arts and crafts; there are fine wines and porcelain on sale in the French village; Oriental goodies in China and Japan; and classic cashmere knitwear and Scottish tartans from the United Kingdom.

Epcot Entertainment
Throughout the day, shows, parades and cultural events take place around the park. Check current park guides for details of Mariachi concerts in Mexico, acrobats in Morocco, operetta in Italy and Caledonian bagpipe serenades in Canada. After dark, the 40-acre (16-ha) World Showcase Lagoon is the scene of the dramatic IllumiNations Reflections of Earth firework, laser light and sound spectacular, visible for miles around.

✈ 72A3
✉ World Drive, Walt Disney World Resort
☎ (407) 824 4321
🕐 Check current schedules

Transportation to the Magic Kingdom

🚌 Shuttle buses pick up and drop off regularly at Transportation and Ticket Center

⛴ Ferry crosses Seven Seas Lagoon into Park; also monorail from Transportation and Ticket Center

Fireworks
You've planned your trip for a while, so reward yourself by staying late to watch "Wishes", the super spectacular fireworks presentation over Cinderella Castle. Narrated by Jimmy Cricket, the 12-minute show features more than 650 fireworks, each timed to explode in sync with a glorious music track. Main Street's a great vantage point; the best is the second floor of the Main Street station. Get there early.

MAGIC KINGDOM ✪✪✪

The Disney theme park that nobody wants to miss is, as a result, the most crowded, overwhelming and deserving of a second visit if you have time. Dominated by the fulsomely turreted and spired fairytale folly of Cinderella Castle, seven themed lands spread out over the 100-acre (40-ha) site, and there are 40-plus adventure attractions, dozens of daily shows, and Disney characters at every turn.

Adventureland Lush tropical plants and eclectic colonial architecture set the scene for some of the adventures in the park. Explore the ingenious Swiss Family Treehouse, laid out amid the branches of a giant (plastic) banyan tree, and grab a pith helmet from the explorers' outfitters for a gentle rainforest Jungle Cruise (FP), which is one of the park's must-see attractions. The fast-talking skippers deliver a series of snappy one-liners on the ten-minute cruise to create an unforgettably fun adventure. Next door, the excellent Pirates of the Caribbean adventure is a rollicking boat journey into pirate territory with noisy special effects, Audio-Animatronics buccaneers, caves full of plundered loot and a marine attack on a Caribbean island. On a less bloodthirsty note, kids will love dodging the waterspewing camels on The Magic Carpets of Aladdin, and singing totem poles and flowers join feathered Audio-Animatronic friends in saccharine sweet renditions of songs from South Seas musicals in The Enchanted Tiki Room (FP).

Fantasyland Gathered at the foot of Cinderella Castle, rides and shows are based on storybook characters designed to appeal to smaller children. Classic fairground rides include the prancing, gilded horses of Cinderella's Golden Carrousel, the whirlygig cups and saucers of the Mad Tea Party and the two-man pachyderms of Dumbo the Flying Elephant. Children can enjoy The Many Adventures of Winnie the Pooh (FP); cool off playing in the waterspouts at Ariel's Grotto; or float through the excruciatingly cute It's a Small World singing doll exhibit. Mickey's PhilharMagic is a thoroughly entertaining 3-D film where Donald Duck takes a wild ride through scenes with Aladdin, Ariel (Little Mermaid) and Simba

Photograph: © Disney

(Lion King); 4-D sensations include splashes of water, gusts of wind and pleasing scents.

Frontierland A step back in time to the Old West with stores, a shooting gallery and good thrill rides. The runaway log flume action at Splash Mountain (FP) kicks up enough of a wave to cool off onlookers, while the Big Thunder Mountain Railroad (FP) takes passengers on a whoopin' and hollerin' roller-coaster ride. Motorised rafts potter across to Tom Sawyer Island.

Liberty Square A genteel counterpoint to the bedlam of the neighboring Frontierland, Liberty Square has a more East Coast colonial feel and a patriotic spreading live oak, known as the Liberty Tree. Here, the Hall of Presidents presentation tackles American history in a series of lectures delivered by Audio-Animatronics US presidents. More lively by far are the undead in the Haunted Mansion (FP). This schlock-horror attraction through curtains of cobwebs, rattling bones and shrieking holograms is more rib-tickling than scary, but it's worth braving the lines. In addition, there are boat trips on the Liberty Belle Riverboat.

Shows and Parades

Tribute shows in the Castle Forecourt and Fantasyland several times a day. Daily, all-singing, all-dancing parade on Main Street, USA at 3pm. Check schedules for the SpectroMagic nighttime parade and Fantasy in the Sky Fireworks (daily).

Disney is bringing in other shows from other Disney parks around the world to help celebrate its 50th anniversary in something called "The Happiest Celebration on Earth." Among these is Cinderellabration, which features Disney princesses in a stage spectacular.

Enjoying a trip on the Liberty Belle Riverboat

Transportation within the Magic Kingdom

🚂 Walt Disney World Railroad circles the perimeter of the park, starting at main entrance, with stops at Frontierland and Mickey's Toontown Fair.
Tomorrowland Transit Authority loop ride operates within Tomorrowland

Cartoon Characters

✉ Disney Character Greeting Locations, highlighted on free map guides

🍴 Character dining at The Crystal Palace (Main Street); Liberty Tree Tavern (dinner only, Liberty Square); character breakfasts in Fantasyland at Cinderella's Royal Table (reservations from the City Hall information centre). For schedules and reservations:
☎ (407) 939 3463

Opposite: *Adventureland includes the ride The Magic Carpets of Aladdin*

Main Street, U.S.A. A prettified Victorian street scene, said to have been inspired by Walt Disney's childhood home in Marceline, Missouri, this broad avenue leads from the front gate up to Cinderella Castle at the hub of the park. Near the gates, in Town Square, City Hall is the main information center and depot for the horse-drawn carriages and trams that trundle up Main Street to the castle. The square also has tree-shaded areas where regular concerts are held by the Main Street Rythm Rascals. All along the route to the castle, shops sell a variety of Disney merchandise and gifts. If just arriving at the park has whetted your appetite, there's an ice-cream parlor and a bake shop.

Mickey's Toontown Fair Home to Mickey and Minnie, this colorful corner of the park is a huge favorite with little children. Take a tour around Minnie's Country House—a veritable symphony in lilac and pink hearts and flowers with a garden to match. Mickey's Country House, next door, as you might expect, displays wardrobes full of the signature red trousers, black jackets and big boots and Pluto's dog kennel is in the garden. Children can cool off in the Donald's Boat play area, thoughtfully equipped with a bungee-soft floor and water jets; and there are pint-sized thrills to be had on The Barnstormer at Goofy's Wiseacre Farm roller-coaster.

Tomorrowland Dramatically updated and revamped, but top of the list here is still Space Mountain (FP), a terrific roller-coaster ride in the dark that many rate as the top ride in the park. Tomorrowland Indy Speedway is enduringly popular, too. Stitch's Great Escape! puts you on the trail of the wild, loveable alien. You join the Galactic Federation to capture Stitch, which is simply a storyline designed to introduce blackouts, weird noises and occasionally scary sensations. Further into Tomorrowland, there are more interactive thrills aboard Buzz Lightyear's Space Ranger Spin (FP) as riders battle the evil Zurg with lasers.

On a rather gentler note, do not miss The Timekeeper, an amusing CircleVision 360° time-travel romp hosted by a duo of smart-talking robots. Take flight in the Astro Orbiter, a mini-rocket ship ride that resembles a chunk of 1950s space cartoon hardware, but does afford a good view of the area, as does the Tomorrowland Transit Authority, which detours into the bowels of Space Mountain to listen to the roller-coaster passengers' screams. Debuted way back at the 1964 New York World's Fair, Walt Disney's Carousel of Progress has its share of loyal fans, but in truth this stilted Audio-Animatronics nostalgia-fest is unlikely to appeal to anybody under 60.

Other Walt Disney World Resort Attractions

BLIZZARD BEACH ★★

Watersports are the specialty of Blizzard Beach, a northern ski-resort-gone-tropical water park, where the chair lifts sport sun umbrellas and the slalom course is a waterslide.

The 60-acre (24-ha) site boasts a dozen different adventure zones in the shadow of "snow-covered" Mount Gushmore. Take a chair lift up to the 60mph (97kph) Summit Plummet slide, or the slightly less dramatic Slush Gusher. Other top attractions include the Teamboat Springs white-water raft ride, inner tubing down Runoff Rapids, and the Snow Stormers flumes.

On a less frenetic note, lazy Cross Country Creek circles the park and a sandy beach borders the wave pool below Mt. Gushmore. Little children can play safely at Tike's Peak; and there is shopping for essentials and souvenirs in The Village, at the east end of the beach.

DISNEY'S FORT WILDERNESS ★★

Disney's Fort Wilderness offers an enormous range of outdoor activities, from watersports to horseback-riding. There are fishing trips for largemouth bass and a children's excursion for bluegill (ages 6–12). Joggers can pound around the 2.5-mile (4-km) jogging trail. Canoes and bicycles are available for rental; sign up for a game of volleyball or basketball; or just work on a tan down at the lakeside beach. Young children also enjoy the petting zoo.

DOWNTOWN DISNEY ★★★

On the shores of Lake Buena Vista, the ever-expanding Downtown Disney shopping, dining and entertainment complex encompasses three distinct districts: the Marketplace; Pleasure Island (► below); and the rapidly expanding West Side attractions area.

Down on the lakeside, the Marketplace combines a selection of colorful boutiques and souvenir shopping outlets (► 104, 106) with a handful of restaurants, including the landmark Rainforest Café (► 99), crowned by a smoking volcano. During the day there are pedalboats for rental from the dock.

The neon-lit West Side boasts the state-of-the-art DisneyQuest interactive games attraction, a 24-screen cinema complex, Virgin Records Megastore, and the Cirque du Soleil, a 1,650-seat theater which stages glitzy, high-energy acrobatic and modern dance productions. Notable dining and entertainment venues include

---

🔢 72A1

✉ W Buena Vista Drive, Walt Disney World Resort

☎ (407) 934 7639

🕐 Daily 10–7 (extended summer and hols)

🍴 Lottawatta Lodge ($–$$), Avalunch and The Warming Hut snack bars ($)

♿ Few

💰 Expensive (or available as option with Park Hopper Plus Pass)

↔ Disney-MGM Studios (► 77–79)

🔢 72B2

✉ Disney's Fort Wilderness Resort and Campground, N Fort Wilderness Trail, Walt Disney World Resort

☎ (407) 824 2900

🕐 Daily 10–5 (extended summer and hols)

🍴 Pop's Place ($)

♿ Few

🔢 72B2

✉ E Buena Vista Drive, Walt Disney World Resort

☎ (407) 828 30581

🕐 Daily. Most shops stay open until 11pm or midnight; restaurants until midnight or 2am

♿ Good

💰 Free. Admission charged to DisneyQuest and for concerts and shows

↔ Pleasure Island (► below)

❓ Information and reservations for Cirque du Soleil, ☎ (407) 939 7600; DisneyQuest (407) 828 4600

Orlando outposts of the House of Blues, Planet Hollywood, Wolfgang Puck Café and Gloria Estefan's Bongos Cuban Café.

PLEASURE ISLAND ✪✪✪

A 6-acre (2.5-ha) nighttime entertainment complex, Pleasure Island's one-off admission ticket entitles guests to party the night away in any or all of its eight night clubs. There is also shopping, dining, movie theaters and dancing in the streets. Several of the shops are open during the day, when admission is free, but the real action (and paid admission) starts at 7pm and builds to a midnight New Year's Eve Street Party, complete with fireworks and a

Pleasure Island has the nightlife scene covered

➕ 72B2

✉ E Buena Vista Drive, Walt Disney World Resort

☎ (407) 939 2648

🕐 Daily, shops 10am–1am; clubs 7pm–2am

🍴 Light dining in the clubs ($$), also access to the Marketplace restaurants (➤ 97–99)

♿ Good

✋ Expensive (or available as option with Park Hopper Plus Pass). Additional charge for movie theaters. Occasional additional charge for special shows in specific clubs

↔ Downtown Disney (➤ above)

❓ Under 18s must be accompanied by a parent; for admission to BET Soundstage Club and Mannequins guests must be 21 or older. All guests need passport, driving licence or birth certificate to buy alcohol

Photograph: © Disney

Photograph: © Disney

Shark Reef at Disney's Typhoon Lagoon water park

blizzard of confetti every night of the year. The revelry continues until 2am.

The night clubs run the gamut from The Comedy Warehouse, with its nightly improvisational comedy shows, to the Rock N Roll Beach Club, which serves up live bands and DJs spinning hits from the 1960s up to the present day. Need to unwind after a hectic day? Then check out the laidback sounds in the Pleasure Island Jazz Company. Still got energy to burn? Lava lamps and mirror balls are all the rage at 1970s-style 8TRAX; for more contemporary sounds, hit Motion, Mannequins Dance Palace or the BET Soundstage™ Club for the best in high-energy hip-hop and R&B. For something completely different, sample the interactive comedy and general weirdness on offer at the Adventurers Club.

TYPHOON LAGOON ●●●

An impressive water park with an artfully shipwrecked feel, Typhoon Lagoon's showpiece is the 2.5-acre (1-ha) lagoon with surf-sized 6-ft (2-m) waves rolling onto sandy beaches every 90 seconds. Rocky Mount Mayday is landscaped with flumes and waterslides, and snorkelers can explore the 362,000-gallon salt-water coral reef environment, Shark Reef, inhabited by real tropical fish. For the biggest thrills in the park, though, check out Humunga Kowabunga, an awesome trio of 30-mph (48-kph) water-slides. The Keelhowl Falls Whitewater rafting adventure is also highly recommended; and there is the separate Ketchakidee Creek water playground for little children.

🕂 72B1
✉ Epcot Center Drive, Walt Disney World Resort
☎ (407) 824 4321
🕐 Daily 10–5 (extended summer and hols)
🍴 Leaning Palms ($), Typhoon Tilly's ($)
♿ Few
💷 Expensive (or available as option with Park Hopper Plus Pass)

Where To...

Right: *A young boy meets cartoon characters at the Islands of Adventure, Florida*

91

Orlando

Prices

Prices are approximate, based on a three-course meal for one without drinks and service:

$ = under $15
$$ = $15 to $30
$$$ = over $30

Diamond Ratings

AAA tourism editors evaluate and rate each restaurant on the overall quality of food, sevice, decor and ambience—with extra emphasis given to food and service. Ratings range from one diamond indicating a simple family-oriented establishment to five diamonds indicating an establishment offering superb culinary skills and an ultimate dining experience.

B-Line Diner ($$)

Fun 1950s-style diner in the Peabody Orlando hotel (Dux ► 93, and Peabody Orlando ► 101). Sandwiches, salads, pizzas and milkshakes are served; service is available 24 hours a day, and there is a take-out counter.

✉ Peabody Orlando, 9801 International Drive ☎ (407) 345 4460 🕐 Breakfast, lunch and dinner 🚌 I-Ride, Lynx #42

♦♦♦Bergamo's ($$)

This Italian restaurant serves home-made pasta, fresh seafood dishes, steaks and other hearty dishes, accompanied by singing waiters.

✉ The Mercado, 8445 International Drive ☎ (407) 352 3805 🕐 Dinner only 🚌 I-Ride, Lynx #42

♦♦Café Tu Tu Tango ($)

A jumbled artist's loft-themed dining room with genuine painters daubing away on site. Order from a wide choice of multi-ethnic appetizer-size eats (tapas-style) and sangria.

✉ 8625 International Drive ☎ (407) 248 2222 🕐 Lunch and dinner 🚌 I-Ride, Lynx #42

California Pizza Kitchen($)

Planning a trip to the mall? This innovative pizza chain makes a great re-fuelling stop. Also pastas, salads sups and puds.

✉ The Florida Mall, 8001 S Orange Blossom Trail ☎ (407) 854 5741 Lunch and dinner; ✉ Mall at Millenia, 4200 Conroy Road ☎ (407) 370 2542 Lunch and dinner

♦♦♦ Charley's Steak House ($$)

Voted one of the Top Ten Steak Houses in the US by The Knife & Fork Club of America, Charley's serves. prime aged beef cooked over a wood fire in a specially built pit. There's good seafood, too.

✉ 8255 International Drive ☎ (407) 363 0228 🕐 Dinner only 🚌 I-Ride, Lynx #42

♦♦Charlie's Lobster House ($$)

Fresh Maine lobster served eight different ways, a long menu of straight seafood and tasty variations such as the house specialty Maryland crab cakes. There is a good wine list and live jazz is performed.

✉ The Mercado, 8445 International Drive ☎ (407) 352 6929 🕐 Dinner only 🚌 I-Ride, Lynx #42

♦♦ ♦♦Christini's Ristorante Italiano ($$$)

Gourmet AAA Four-Diamond Italian restaurant. Classical cuisine with some light modern touches; one of the chef's star turns is *fettucini alla Christini* and another specialty is the 26oz veal chop. Smart dress; charming service.

✉ The Marketplace, 7600 Dr Phillips Boulevard/Sand Lake Road ☎ (407) 345 8770 🕐 Dinner only

♦♦♦Le Coq au Vin ($$–$$$)

This one is something of a rarity: a Central Florida French restaurant that has a long-standing reputation for producing well-prepared classics in a relaxing atmosphere. Inside a cozy renovated home.

✉ 4800 S Orange Avenue ☎ (407) 851 6980 🕐 Tue–Sun

lunch and dinner

Damon's The Place for Ribs ($$)

An old favorite for no-nonsense barbecued fare. Mouth-watering, juicy ribs are served up with the house special sauce and prime aged beef.

✉ The Mercado/Suite 108, 8445 International Drive
☎ (407) 352 5984 🕐 Mon–Fri lunch only, Sat–Sun open 3pm–10pm 🚌 I-Ride, Lynx #42

Dexter's of Thornton Park ($$)

Just a few blocks east of downtown Orlando in trendy Thornton Park, this eclectic neighborhood meeting place is popular with young professionals and local residents. Dine inside or at the sidewalk café. Dishes include a variety of creative soups, pastas, salads and entrees.

✉ 808 East Washington Street
☎ (407) 648 2777 🕐 Lunch and dinner

Dux ($$$)

The Peabody Orlando's award-winning signature restaurant. Elegant décor, sophisticated New American cuisine and an excellent wine cellar are all part of the package. (Jackets for men.)

✉ Peabody Orlando, 9801 International Drive ☎ (407) 345 4550 🕐 Mon–Sat, dinner only 🚌 I-Ride, Lynx #42

Emeril's Restaurant Orlando ($$$)

America's most popular chef brought his name and skills to this eatery at CityWalk, where a wonderful mix of Old World and Louisiana cooking meet with dishes like oven-baked pizzas to rack of lamb to ham crusted snapper. One of the most upscale restaurants at any theme park, anywhere.

✉ Universal CityWalk
☎ (407) 224 2424 🕐 Lunch and dinner

Flippers Pizza ($)

Well-priced local pizza chain specializing in hand-tossed, made-to-order pizzas, baked pasta dishes, salads and dips.

✉ 4774 Kirkman Road
☎ (407) 521 0607;
✉ 7480 Universal Boulevard
☎ (407) 351 5643 🕐 Lunch and dinner

The Globe ($–$$)

If you find yourself downtown, here's a place that's hip and trendy and right across from the Orange County Historical Museum. Open very early to very late, sandwiches and salads as popular as the open air setting, and many dishes reflect clever twists on classic dishes from around the globe.

✉ 25 Wall Street Court
☎ (407) 849 9904 🕐 Lunch and dinner

Hard Rock Café ($$)

An Orlando outpost for the world's largest Hard Rock Café at Universal Studios, next to the Hard Rock Live auditorium. The dining area contains the usual display of rock memorabilia including Elvis's Gibson guitar and the Beatles' 1960s suits. The menu has all-American burgers, hickory-smoked barbecue chicken, salads and the charmingly named Pig Sandwich.

✉ Universal's CityWalk
☎ (407) 351 7625 🕐 Lunch and dinner

Dux Delight

Ever since a couple of well-refreshed hunters jokingly popped their live decoy ducks in the fountain of the Peabody Memphis over a century ago, the Peabody people have had a thing for ducks. Twice daily (11am and 5pm) The Peabody Orlando's marching mallards parade through the main lobby between their daily duties of circling the fountain and their $100,000 Royal Duck Palace. Take afternoon tea—and a camera! (➤ 101)

Create Your Own

Want to create a popular restaurant? Try out the idea in Orlando. Restaurant corporations around America have learned that the wide range of tastes and nationalities tourists bring to Orlando mean they can custom-craft a menu that appeals to a wide range of diners. National chains Red Lobster, Olive Garden, Bahama Breeze (► 97) and Smokey Bones BBQ started right here.

🍷🍷 Jimmy Buffett's Margaritaville ($$)

A casual Key West-style eatery and bar that serves up mega cheeseburgers, namesake margaritas and a side order of Jimmy Buffett tunes.

✉ Universal's CityWalk
☎ (407) 224 2155 🕐 Lunch and dinner

🍷🍷 🍷🍷 Manuel's on the 28th ($$$)

Downtown's most exclusive dining room with spectacular views from the 28th floor of the NationsBank Center. Sophisticated continental-"Floribbean" cuisine. Jackets preferred.

✉ 390 N Orange Avenue ☎ (407) 246 6580 🕐 Dinner only

🍷🍷🍷 Ming Court ($$$)

Stylish Chinese restaurant with views over manicured Oriental gardens, mini waterfalls and koi ponds. Very good fresh seafood, and there are steaks and grills as well as skillfully prepared Chinese cuisine.

✉ 9188 International Drive
☎ (407) 351 9988 🕐 Lunch and dinner 🚌 I-Ride, Lynx #42

🍷🍷 Motown Cafe ($$)

Celebrating some of America's favorite music with downhome stick-to-the-ribs dishes. Dine on soul food and Southern fried foods while perusing a collection of Motown memorabilia and watching occasional floor shows.

✉ Universal CityWalk
☎ (407) 224 2500 🕐 Lunch and dinner

🍷🍷 Numero Uno ($)

Small and friendly Latin American restaurant with generous portion control and a hearty menu of filling staples from paella Valencia to roast pork and black beans, steaks and seafood.

✉ 2499 S Orange Avenue
☎ (407) 841 3840 🕐 Lunch and dinner. Closed Sun

🍷🍷 Race Rock ($$)

Motor racing memorabilia and rock music in a heaven-sent dining opportunity for boy racers (► 95, panel). First-class pizzas, pasta, burgers and chicken wings.

✉ 8986 International Drive
☎ (407) 248 9876 🕐 Lunch and dinner 🚌 I-Ride, Lunx #42

🍷🍷 Ran-Getsu of Tokyo ($$$)

Authenic Japanese cuisine and an attractive location overlooking a Japanese garden and koi pond. Chefs prepare traditional sushi, sukiyaki and tempura. Entertainment at weekends.

✉ 8400 International Drive
☎ (407) 345 0044 🕐 Dinner only 🚌 I-Ride, Lynx #42

🍷🍷🍷 Roy's ($$–$$$)

One of Orlando's gourmet hot spots. Chef Greg Richie blends western techniques, Asian ingredients and a dash of Hawaiian inspiration to create great fusion cuisine.

✉ 7760 W Sand Lake Road
☎ (407) 352 4844 🕐 Dinner only 🚌 I-Ride, Lynx #42

🍷🍷🍷 Samba Room ($$)

A Latin café with rhythm and South American–Caribbean panache. Cocktails and spiced rums, seafood, grilled meats, exotic fruits and the Bossa Nova.

✉ 7468 W Sand Lake Road
☎ (407) 226 0550 or l-800 713 9106 🕐 Lunch and dinner 🚌 I-Ride, Lynx #42

Around Orlando

Kissimmee

🍷Giordano's of Kissimmee ($–$$)

Always busy with visitors and locals, this family-friendly Chicago-style pizzeria also servies a selection of other favorite Italian dishes. Also at Lake Buena Vista.

✉ **7866 W Irlo Bronson Memorial Highway/US192** ☎ **(407) 397 0044;** ✉ **12151 S Apopka-Vineland Road, Lake Buena Vista** ☎ **(407) 239 8900** 🕐 **Lunch and dinner**

🍷🍷Key W Kool's Oak Grill ($$)

Nautical décor with a nod towards the Florida Keys and a steak and seafood grill menu fresh from the oakwood pit barbecue.

✉ **7725 W US192 (west of I-4)** ☎ **(407) 239 7166** 🕐 **Dinner only**

🍷🍷Pacino's ($$)

Family-owned modern trattoria serving home-made bread and operettas, good pasta dishes, seafood and other Italian favorites.

✉ **5795 W US192** ☎ **(407) 396 8022** 🕐 **Lunch and dinner**

Lake Wales

Chalet Suzanne ($$$)

Award-winning restaurant in a lovely country inn, Chalet Suzanne's cozy, antique-filled dining room overlooks a small lake. The excellent American-Continental menu is short, the wine list long, the service attentive.

✉ **3800 Chalet Suzanne Drive (off CR17A, 4.5 miles (7km) north of Lake Wales)** ☎ **(863) 676 6011 or 1-800 433 6011** 🕐 **Lunch and dinner. Closed Mon**

Longwood

🍷🍷🍷Enzo's on the Lake ($$–$$$)

Elegant Italian dining room with a thoroughly Mediterranean feel in a converted house overlooking Lake Fairy. Fish soup with crab and *buccatin alla Enzo* (pasta with a robust mushroom-bacon-pea sauce) are the delicious house specialties.

✉ **1130 S US17-92** ☎ **(407) 834 9872** 🕐 **Dinner, lunch Fri only**

Maitland

🍷🍷Buca di Beppo ($$)

One of the most creative Italian restaurants anywhere, with photos, artwork and memorabilia crowding every wall space. Entrees are prepared to be shared among everyone—order a plate of spaghetti and you can feed a family of four. Clever, creative, and lots of fun—although a bit far from the tourist areas.

✉ **1351 S Orlando Avenue** ☎ **(407) 622 7663** 🕐 **Dinner only**

🍷🍷Melting Pot ($$)

A fondue restaurant that's managed to survive in an out-of-the-way location for more than 25 years; located in Maitland, about 45 minutes from Disney. The attraction here is dishes you can prepare and cook yourself atop a small stove at your table. Follow up a combination platter with white chocolate amaretto fondue topped by an array of fresh fruits. You'll never leave hungry.

✉ **500 E Horatio Avenue** ☎ **(407) 628 1134** 🕐 **Dinner only**

Race Rock

Dine in the fast lane at this landmark racing-themed restaurant with a distinctive chequered flag roof (► 94). Celebrity partners include Richard and Kyle Petty, Michael Andretti and Don Prudhomme. The foyer is a monument to high-octane horsepower decked out with Formula One and Indy cars, dragsters, motorcycles, and speedboats. Video screens show racing footage, there are video games and, of course, a chance to stock up on Race Rock merchandise.

Cutting the Cost

Your vacation money can go a lot further when you know where to shop—buying all your food at the theme parks can make you very broke, very fast. So for film, snacks, candy, personal hygiene items and nearly everything you need, ask for directions to some of these local and national stores:

Wal-Mart: The global behemoth that sells practically everything at competitive prices.

Publix: The largest supermarket chain in Orlando.

Walgreens: A popular drugstore (each with a pharmacy) that also sells vacation staples like film, souvenirs, snacks, make-up, magazines, candy and much more.

CVS: Walgreen's rival, with a similar—and slightly more expensive—inventory.

Mount Dora

♛♛♛Goblin Market ($$)

Inside it feels like a private library, which makes this restaurant appealing to romantics and friends who enjoy settling back to enjoy good company and conversation. Entrees are artfully presented spins on beef, pork, lamb, poultry and seafood.

✉ **330 Dora Drawdy Lane**
☎ **(352) 735 0059** 🕐 **Lunch and dinner**

♛♛Windsor Rose English Tea Room ($)

Welcoming tea room with a gift and garden shop attached. Traditional Cornish pasties, Scotch eggs and Ploughman's (bread and cheese) lunches, as well as home-made cakes and biscuits.

✉ **144 W 4th Avenue** ☎ **(352) 735 2551** 🕐 **Morning coffee, lunch and tea**

Winter Park

♛Brandywine's Deli ($)

A cute and intimate deli right on Winter Park's popular Park Avenue. People watch while dining on hearty sandwiches, diet plates, and light fare.

✉ **505 North Park Avenue**
☎ **(407) 647 0055** 🕐 **Lunch and dinner**

♛♛Briar Patch ($)

This is another Park Avenue favorite that serves fresh country-style breakfast, lunch and dinner dishes as well as delicious desserts. A nice spot to take a break from your shopping excursion.

✉ **252 North Park Avenue**
☎ **(407) 645 4566**
🕐 **Breakfast, lunch and dinner**

♛Bubbalou's Bodacious Bar-B-Que ($)

A local favorite for down-home BBQ sandwiches and platters. Nothing fancy, just good BBQ cooking a short drive from Winter Park's Park Avenue and the Winter Park Village shopping mall.

✉ **1471 Lee Road**
☎ **(407) 628 1212** 🕐 **Lunch and dinner**

♛♛Cheesecake Factory ($–$$)

Don't let the name fool you—in addition to cheesecake, there are countless types of cuisines served in a warm, fun and active atmosphere. Located at the Winter Park Village, a popular shopping and entertainment area.

✉ **520 North Orlando Avenue**
☎ **(407) 644-4220** 🕐 **Lunch and dinner**

Panera Bread ($)

A great lunch stop close to Rollins College. This bakery-cum-café chain is hugely popular and good value. Tuck into homemade soup in a sourdough bread bowl, sandwiches, salads and frothy cappuccinos with a pastry on the side. Also at other locations.

✉ **118 W Fairbanks Avenue**
☎ **(407) 645 3939**
🕐 **Breakfast, lunch and dinner**

♛♛♛Park Plaza Gardens ($$$)

An elegant New Orleans-style covered courtyard provides the setting for award-winning Florida cuisine. Creative dishes are served, employing the freshest local ingredients, there is a fine wine list and the service is exemplary.

Sunday brunch is a local institution.

⊠ **111 East Lyman Avenue**
☎ **(407) 645 2475** 🕐 **Lunch and dinner**

🍷Powerhouse Café ($)

A few steps from the shopping district of Park Avenue, this little hole in the wall features organic health foods, smoothies, soups and salads in a casual, creative, student-friendly setting.

⊠ **111 East Lyman Avenue**
☎ **(407) 645 3616** 🕐 **Lunch and dinner only**

Walt Disney World Resort and Lake Buena Vista

🍷🍷🍷🍷Arthur's 27 ($$$)

International cuisine, elegant surroundings and panoramic views over the Walt Disney World Resort nighttime firework displays. A choice of *prix-fixe* menus as well as à *la carte* specialties. Reservations advised.

⊠ **Wyndham Palace Resort & Spa, 1900 Buena Vista Drive**
☎ **(407) 827 3450 or 1-800 327 2990** 🕐 **Dinner only**

🍷🍷🍷Artist Point ($$–$$$)

Hearty cooking from the Pacfic Northwest fits right in with the Wilderness Lodge décor. Salmon, Penn Cove mussels, game dishes and a notable wine list. The restaurant hosts the very popular Character Breakfast, where kids can eat while meeting their favorite characters in person.

⊠ **Disney's Wilderness Lodge, Magic Kingdom Resort Area**
☎ **(407) 939 3463**
🕐 **Breakfast and dinner**

🍷🍷Bahama Breeze ($$)

Created and developed in Orlando, this small chain is destined to expand with its creative and zesty Caribbean takes on chicken, fish and steak dishes. An outdoor patio with live island-style entertainment is another plus. Expect a wait.

⊠ **8735 Vineland Avenue, Lake Buena Vista** ☎ **(407) 938-9010**
⊠ **8849 International Drive**
☎ **(407) 248 2499** 🕐 **Lunch and dinner**

🍷🍷Bongos Cuban Café ($$–$$$)

Restaurant and nightclub created by Miami's disco queen, Gloria Estefan, and husband Emilio. Authentic Cuban-Latin American music and food.

⊠ **Downtown Disney West Side** ☎ **(407) 828 0999**
🕐 **Lunch and dinner**

🍷🍷🍷California Grill ($$)

Stylish Californian cuisine with views over the Magic Kingdom. Watch the delicious designer pizzas, oak-fired beef tenderloin and seared tuna steaks being prepared in the open-to-view kitchen.

⊠ **Disney's Contemporary Resort, Magic Kingdom Resort Area** ☎ **(407) 939 3463**
🕐 **Dinner only**

Chefs de France ($$$)

A triumvirate of top French chefs (Bocuse, Vergé and Lenôtre) provided the creative inspiration behind this upscale restaurant in Epcot's World Showcase. The candles, crystal and elegance make it look and feel like the Champs Elysee. Reservations are a must.

⊠ **Epcot , Epcot Center Drive**
☎ **(407) 939 3463** 🕐 **Lunch and dinner**

Disney Character Dining

A sure-fire hit with children, there are plenty of opportunities to dine out with favorite cartoon characters. Minnie Mouse hosts breakfast at the Ohana in Disney's Polynesian Resort; Winnie the Pooh, Eeyore and Tigger tuck in at The Crystal Palace Buffet in Magic Kingdom; and Admiral Goofy and crew attend the Cape May Café breakfast buffet at the Disney Beach Club Resort. Check schedules and make reservations for these and other sightings (☎ (407) 939 3463). See also ► 86.

Rainforest Café

A smoking, 65-ft (20-m) high mini-volcano in the middle of Downtown Disney? Unbelievable. But then so is the Rainforest Café, brainchild of Steven Schussler, entrepreneur and eco-warrior, who once moved all the furniture out of his house to improve the environment for his pet parrots. Immersed in the simulated rainforest, marvel at the live and animated wildlife, feel the creeping mist and be assured that all the ingredients are environmentally correct.

♛♛Cinderella's Royal Table ($$)

For an unforgettable experience, make a reservation and enjoy dining inside Cinderella Castle. Yes, the Castle. Dishes include prime rib, beef pie, roast chicken, barbecue and other comfort foods. Arrive early and the kids can enjoy a Disney character breakfast.

✉ **Magic Kingdom** ☎ **(407) 939 3463** ◷ **Lunch and dinner**

♛♛Fulton's Crab House ($$$)

Housed in a replica turn-of-the-last-century riverboat permanently moored to the shore of Lake Buena Vista, this seafood restaurant is popular, so be prepared to have to wait for dinner. It's usually worth it for the enormous choice of expertly prepared fresh fish, a raw bar, and a notable sour cherry cobbler for dessert.

✉ **Downtown Disney Marketplace, 1670 E Buena Vista Drive** ☎ **(407) 934 2628** ◷ **Lunch and dinner**

The Garden Grill ($$)

Near the food court inside The Land pavilion at Epcot, this table service restaurant features character meals at breakfast and lunch. As you dine, you'll slowly spin past nature scenes. Oh, some of the items on your plate were grown right here.

✉ **Epcot, The Land** ☎ **(407) 939 3463** ◷ **Lunch and dinner**

The Hollywood Brown Derby ($$)

A faithful recreation of Hollywood's famous Brown Derby restaurant, featuring comfortable 1930s-style décor.

✉ **Disney-MGM Studios, W Buena Vista Drive** ☎ **(407) 939 3463** ◷ **Lunch and dinner**

♛♛♛♛Jiko ($$)

The signature restaurant of Disney's elegant and intimate Animal Kingdom Lodge, this restaurant defines its dishes as New African—traditional African dishes with influences from other cultures. Colorful décor, exemplary service and creative cuisine. Make a night of it.

✉ **Animal Kingdom Lodge, Lake Buena Vista** ☎ **(407) 938 3000** ◷ **Dinner only**

L'Originale Alfredo di Roma Ristorante ($$–$$$)

One of the stars in Epcot's culinary crown and very popular. Sample the namesake *fettucine alfredo*, seafood, veal dishes and Italian wines, all served to the sound of the singing waiters.

✉ **World Showcase, Epcot, Epcot Center Drive** ☎ **(407) 939 3463** ◷ **Lunch and dinner**

♛♛♛Palio ($$–$$)

Fine dining restaurant where hearty Northern Italian dishes are the backbone of the menu; *osso buco* with saffron risotto, *piccata alla Milanese* and a beef fillet with polenta and shallots. The setting is taken from the Palio horse race in Siena and includes colorful flags.

✉ **1200 Epcot Resorts Blvd** ☎ **(407) 934 1610** ◷ **Dinner only**

♛♛Pebbles ($$–$$$)

Creative New American cuisine for the "casual gourmet." Delicious salads, seafood and poultry in a relaxed atmosphere. There is a second outpost in downtown's Church Street district. (► 94)

📧 **Crossroads Shopping Center 12551 SR535** ☎ **(407) 827 1111** 🕐 **Lunch and dinner;** 📧 **17 W Church Street** ☎ **(407) 839 0892**

🍷🍷Portobello Yacht Club ($$–$$$)

Generous Northern Italian cooking, featuring mountains of home-made pasta, pizzas cooked in a wood-burning brick oven and daily specials with the emphasis on fresh seafood. Bustling casual atmosphere and waterfront terrace dining overlooking Lake Buena Vista.

📧 **Downtown Disney (just outside Pleasure Island), 1650 E Buena Vista Drive** ☎ **(407) 934 8888** 🕐 **Lunch and dinner**

Prime Time Café ($–$$)

You'll feel like you're on television in this fun 50's TV sitcom-themed restaurant located at the Disney-MGM Studios. A TV mom takes your order and serves up home-type specialties and soda fountain drinks and asks you to join the "Clean Plate Club."

📧 **Disney-MGM Studios** ☎ **(407) 939 3463** 🕐 **Lunch and dinner**

Rainforest Café ($$–$$$)

Enormously popular jungle-themed restaurant swathed with trees and waterfalls, parrots and piña coladas. Choose from a broad menu of American favorites with a Caribbean twist (► 98, panel). Also at Animal Kingdom.

📧 **Downtown Disney Marketplace, 1800 E Buena**

Vista Drive ☎ **(407) 827 8500** 🕐 **Lunch and dinner**

🍷🍷Restaurant Marrakesh ($$)

Enjoy Moroccan cuisine in a recreation of a royal palace with mosaic tile work and inlaid ceilings. Belly dancers and musicians perform regularly throughout the day.

📧 **Epcot, Moroccan Pavilion** ☎ **(407) 939 3463** 🕐 **Lunch and dinner**

Rose and Crown ($)

If you miss your favorite pub, drop in at Epcot's recreation where Americans and Brits belly up to the bar for beers, ales and traditional English pub fare. Outside, a dining patio overlooks the lagoon.

📧 **Epcot, United Kingdom Pavilion** ☎ **(407) 939 3463** 🕐 **Lunch only**

🍷🍷Spoodles ($–$$)

Appetizing Mediterranean menu from wood-fired thin-crust pizzas to Greek *mezes*, North African houmous, kebabs and salads. Steak and seafood also on offer.

📧 **Disney's Boardwalk, Epcot Resort Area** ☎ **(407) 939 3463** 🕐 **Breakfast and dinner**

🍷🍷🍷🍷Victoria & Alberts ($$$)

For a special, but expensive, treat this intimate restaurant, within Disney's Grand Floridian Resort, is probably Disney's best. The ever-changing menu offers six courses of meticulous and delicious world-class contemporary cuisine, reflecting both American and International influences.

📧 **4401 Grand Floridian Way** ☎ **(407) 939 3463** 🕐 **Dinner only**

Dining with Children

Not surprisingly, most Orlando restaurants welcome children. Family restaurants, burger chains and a wide choice of budget dining options abound around the International Drive resort area and Kissimmee. Many smarter restaurants are equally child-friendly and discounted children's menus are widely available; if you don't see one on display always ask.

For reservations at any Disney restaurant or Dinner Show call (407) WDW-DINE or (407) 939 3463

Orlando

Prices

The following price bands are given on a per night minimum for a standard room regardless of single, double or multi-person occupancy:

$ = under $60
$$ = $60 to $120
$$$ = over $120

It is worth noting that many Orlando hotels make no additional charge for children with their parents.

Diamond Ratings

AAA tourism editors evaluate and rate each lodging establishment based on the overall quality and services. AAA's diamond rating criteria reflect the design and service standards set by the lodging industry, combined with the expectations of its members.

A one or two diamond rating represents a clean and well-maintained property offering comfortable rooms, with the two diamond property showing enhancements in decor and furnishings. A three diamond property shows marked upgrades in physical attributes, services and comfort and may offer additional amenities. A four diamond rating signifies a property offering a high level of service and hospitality and a wide variety of amenities and upscale facilities. A five diamond rating represents a world-class facility, offering the highest level of luxurious accommodations and personalized guest services.

▼▼▼▼Ameri Suites ($$)

Well-priced suite hotel close to Universal Orlando. Living-dining area and separate bedroom, with kitchen, pool, exercise room and breakfast buffet. Bus to attractions.

✉ **5895 Caravan Court** ☎ **(407) 351 0627 or 1-800 833 1516**

▼▼▼▼Best Western Plaza International ($$)

Well-equipped chain hotel midway down International Drive; 672 rooms and suites; pool; dining; airport bus.

✉ **8738 International Drive** ☎ **(407) 345 8195 or 1-800 654 7160** 🚌 **I-Ride, Lynx #42**

▼▼▼Best Western Universal Inn ($$)

A short drive from Universal, 70 single-room units feature coffeemakers, irons, hair dryers and some with refrigerators and microwaves. A free expanded continental breakfast adds to the value.

✉ **5618 Vineland Road** ☎ **(407) 226 9119**

▼▼▼Clarion Hotel Universal ($$)

Near Wet 'n' Wild and tourist-friendly International Drive, 298 rooms are standard one-bedroom units with the added bonus of free local calls. The hotel features two restaurants, a cocktail lounge, coin laundry, heated pool, whirlpools, a lighted tennis court and basketball.

✉ **7299 Universal Boulevard** ☎ **(407) 351 5009 or 1-800 445-7299**

▼▼▼Comfort Inn International ($$)

A safe bet on I-Drive, with refrigerators, coffeemakers and, for a fee, high-speed Internet connection. If the outdoor pool's not enough to keep you fit, an off-site health club is available for a fee. Breakfast, phone calls, and transportations to Universal are free.

✉ **8134 International Drive** ☎ **(407) 313 4000** 🚌 **I-Ride, Lynx #42**

▼▼▼Doubletree at the Entrance to Universal Orlando ($$)

Reasonably priced rooms and suites (742) near Universal. Amenities include dining and a late night lounge; pool; shopping arcade; kid's playground.

✉ **5780 Major Boulevard** ☎ **(407) 351 1000 or 1-800 373 9855**

▼▼Fairfield Inn by Marriott ($–$$)

Quiet corner close to I-Drive and dining options. 135 spotless, comfortable rooms; pool, complimentary continental breakfast.

✉ **8342 Jamaican Court** ☎ **(407) 363 1944 or 1-800 228 2800**

▼▼▼Hampton Inn—International Drive Area ($$)

Set back just east of I-Drive. 336 rooms, all with fridge and microwave; pool; complimentary breakfast. Also a second Orlando location, just south of Universal Orlando.

✉ **6101 Sand Lake Road** ☎ **(407) 763 7886 or 1-800 763 1100;**

✉ **7110 S Kirkman Road** ☎ **(407) 345 1112 or 1-800 763 1100**

▼▼Howard Johnson Suites ($$)

Suite hotel near Universal; 96 two-room efficiencies

with kitchen and patio. Swimming pool, spa, fitness center and tennis, plus picnic areas with barbecue grills.

✉ **4601 S Kirkman Road** ☎ **(407) 313 1000 or 1-800 826 8515**

☸☸☸Hyatt Regency Orlando International Airport ($$–$$$)

If you have a very early flight, this is an attractive airport hotel with direct access from the terminal; 446 spacious rooms and suites; restaurants and bar; pool.

✉ **9300 Airport Boulevard** ☎ **(407) 825 1234 or 1-800 233 1234** 🚌 **Lynx #42**

☸☸☸Orlando Embassy Suites International Drive South ($$$)

Well-priced two-room suites sleeping up to six people in a central location. Pools; fitness center; Family Fun Center; complimentary cooked breakfast.

✉ **8978 International Drive** ☎ **(407) 352 1400 or 1-800 433 7275** 🚌 **I-Ride, Lynx #42**

☸☸☸Orlando World Center Marriott ($$$)

A huge resort hotel with 2,000 rooms. Choice of restaurants from fine dining to pizza; pools, 18-hole golf course, lighted tennis courts and health club; good children's facilities, including baby-sitting services.

✉ **8701 World Center Drive** ☎ **(407) 239 4200 or 1-800 621 0638** 🚌 **I-Ride, Lynx #42**

☸☸☸☸The Peabody Orlando ($$$)

High-rise luxury opposite the Convention Center, with 949 attractive and spacious rooms and suites with a view; pool, tennis, health club; golf by arrangement. Restaurants including fine dining at Dux (► 93).

✉ **9801 International Drive** ☎ **(407) 345 4522 or 1-800 423 8257** 🚌 **I-Ride, Lynx #42**

☸☸☸☸Portofino Bay at Universal Orlando ($$$)

Luxurious Italian Riviera-themed complex with a boat to transport you to the theme parks. There are 750 lovely rooms; a dining area, waterfront boats, swimming pools and childminding.

✉ **5601 Universal Boulevard** ☎ **(407) 503 1000 or 1-877 819 7884**

☸☸Red Horse Inn ($$)

Moderately priced themed hotel with character. A western feel and standard amenities flow through each of 159 standard units. Activities include shuffleboard and privileges at an off-site health club.

✉ **5825 International Drive** ☎ **(407) 351 4100**

☸☸☸Rosen Plaza Hotel ($$)

Elegant executive-type hotel close to the Convention Center; 800 rooms; pool; restaurants.

✉ **9700 International Drive** ☎ **(407) 996 9700 or 1-800 366 9700** 🚌 **I-Ride, Lynx #42**

☸☸☸Staybridge Suites ($$$)

Convenient for all the sights, as well as for the shopping and dining on I-Drive: 146 one- to three-bed units that can sleep up to eight people. Swimming pool; bar. Also at Lake Buena Vista.

✉ **8480 International Drive** ☎ **(407) 352 2400 or 1-800 833 4353** 🚌 **I-Ride, Lynx #42**

Reserve in Advance

Reservations can be made by phone, fax or mail, and should be made as early as possible. A deposit (usually by credit card) equivalent to the nightly rate will ensure that your room is held until 6pm; if you are arriving later, inform the hotel. Credit card is the preferred payment method; travelers' checks and cash are also acceptable, but payment may have to be made in advance. The final charge will include Florida's 6 percent sales tax and local resort taxes.

Rooms, Suites and Efficiencies

Rooms in American hotels are generally large, with two double beds as standard. Suites, with two or three separate rooms, are increasingly common and are a good option for families. Efficiencies are rooms with a kitchenette, as well as a separate bathroom.

Around Orlando

Spa Treatment
Footsore and weary after a day at Disney? The Wyndham Palace's superb spa has the answer with its special Theme Park Foot Relief Massage. Spa guests (non-hotel residents welcome) can choose from a tempting array of more than 30 face and body treatments, ranging from aromatherapy to mineral baths. Reserve in for a single treatment or a half-day, full-day or weekend of luxurious pampering. Additional facilities include a Fitness Center, saunas, and beauty salon.

Staying at Disney
A few years ago, Walt Disney World saw a lot of their guests dropping in for the day and then leaving to stay at a modestly-priced motel. To fix this, they created Value Resorts; streamlined hotels that may not have all the frills of their grand resorts, but puts guests on site. The rates are competitive with off-property hotels and offer added advantages: free parking, early admission to certain parks, and complimentary transportation to the theme parks, water parks and Downtown Disney. Each of these resorts has a theme, a large pool, restaurant, and clean rooms. Check them out online.

Kissimmee

⚜⚜⚜Clarion Hotel Maingate ($$)
The 198 rooms are on two storys; pool and jacuzzi; fitness center; dining; other restaurants and shopping within walking distance.
✉ **7675 W Irlo Bronson Memorial Highway/US192** ☎ **(407) 396 4000 or 1-800 568 3352**

⚜⚜⚜Comfort Inn-Maingate West ($)
Located just outside Disney, this basic hotel offers a pool, free calls, and a free newspaper. It may not be spectacular, but it's close.
✉ **9330 West Highway 192** ☎ **(863) 424 8420 or 1-800 440-4473**

⚜⚜Days Inn 192 Orlando-Kissimmee ($)
A large hotel (174 one-bedroom units) with the requisite heated outdoor pool, game room, coin laundry, and free continental breakfast. Complimentary transportation is available to major attractions.
✉ **4104 West Irlo Bronson Memorial Highway** ☎ **(407) 846 4714**

⚜⚜Econo Lodge Maingate Resort ($–$$)
A budget option earning consistantly good reports. Pool and restaurant, shuttle service, car rental.
✉ **7514 W Irlo Bronson Memorial Highway/US192** ☎ **(407) 396 2000 or 1-800 365 6935**

⚜⚜HoJo Maingate East ($$)
Reasonably spacious rooms (367), including 197 efficiencies with fully equipped kitchens. Two pools and a playground; close to dining and shopping.
✉ **6051 W Irlo Bronson Memorial Highway/US192** ☎ **(407) 396 1748 or 1-800 288 4678**

⚜⚜⚜Homewood Suites by Hilton ($$$)
AAA Three-Diamond 156-suite hotel. Pool and spa; complimentary continental breakfast; pets allowed.
✉ **3100 Parkway Boulevard** ☎ **(407) 396 2229 or 1-888 351 9100**

⚜⚜⚜La Quinta Inn & Suites Kissimmee (Orlando Maingate) ($$)
About 3 miles (5km) from Disney and close to other attractions, this hotel features 132 standard rooms and 16 suites. There's a playground, whirlpool, heated pool, and rooms have refrigerators, microwaves and coffeemakers.
✉ **3484 Polynesian Isle Boulevard** ☎ **(407) 997 1700**

⚜⚜⚜Mainstay Suites and Resort on Lake Cecile ($$)
Very reasonable all-suite resort with 158 units. Fully equipped kitchens (including dishwasher); pool and tennis; bar; laundry.
✉ **4786 W Irlo Bronson Memorial Highway/US192** ☎ **(407) 396 2056 or 1-800 468 3027**

⚜⚜⚜Ramada Inn Resort Maingate ($$)
Full-service resort with 391 rooms on Walt Disney World Resort's doorstep. Pools, basketball courts, tennis and restaurant.
✉ **2950 Reedy Creek Boulevard** ☎ **(407) 396 4466 or 1-800 365 6935**

⚜⚜Tropical Palms Resort ($$)

A family-smart choice of 138 cottages in small groupings, with fishing, playground, basketball, horseshoes, shuffleboard, volleyball and a heated pool. Three night minimum stay required in season. Located near Old Town in Kissimmee.

✉ **2650 Holiday Trail** ☎ **(407) 396 4595 or 1-800 647-2567**

⚜⚜⚜Wonderland Inn ($$)

A bed-and-breakfast option. 11 rooms and suites (some with kitchenettes), plus a cottage in a garden setting. Continental breakfast, wine/cheese hour.

✉ **3601 S Orange Blossom Trail** ☎ **(407) 847 2477 or 1-877 847 2477**

Walt Disney World Resort and Lake Buena Vista

⚜⚜⚜Disney's All-Star Sports, Movies and Music Resorts ($$)

Three good value themed resorts; 5,760 rooms, each able to accommodate four adults; good facilities.

✉ **Animal Kingdom Resort Area** ☎ **(407) 934 7639 or 1-800 647 7900**

⚜⚜ ⚜⚜Disney's BoardWalk Inn and Villas ($$$)

New England-style waterfront resort with 378 rooms and 532 one-, two- and three-bedroom studios and villas sleeping 4–12 adults. Sporting facilities; children's activities; dining and shopping.

✉ **2101 N Epcot Resorts Boulevard** ☎ **(407) 939 5100; reservations (407) 934 7639**

⚜⚜⚜Disney's Port Orleans Resort ($$$)

Mid-range hotel with an attractive New Orleans-style setting providing 1,008 rooms in three-story buildings. A range of activities on offer include swimming, tennis courts and boating; restaurants.

✉ **2201 Orleans Drive** ☎ **(407) 934 5000; reservations (407) 934 7639**

⚜⚜⚜Disney's Fort Wilderness Campground ($)

Woodland camp site offering hook-up facilities and cabins that can sleep six (➤ 90).

✉ **4510 N Fort Wilderness Trail** ☎ **(407) 824 2900; reservations (407) 934 7639**

⚜⚜⚜Doubletree Club Hotel Lake Buena Vista ($$)

Vibrant colors liven up this hotel, which makes it popular with children. Of the 246 units, four are one-bedroom suites. Facilities available include a whirlpool, exercise room, heated pool, wading pool, restaurant, gift shop, and transportation to Disney.

✉ **12490 Apopka-Vineland Road, Lake Buena Vista** ☎ **(407) 239 4646 or 1-800 521-3297**

⚜⚜⚜Wyndham Palace Resort & Spa ($$$)

Luxurious and elegant hotel with 1,013 rooms/suites thoughtfully equipped with spa products (➤ 102, panel). Excellent recreational facilities; children's programs; gourmet dining at Arthur's 27 (➤ 97).

✉ **1900 Buena Vista Drive** ☎ **(407) 827 2727**

Budget Tips

Most hotels offer accommodations in several price ranges. If you are on a budget and the hotel rate offered is at the top end of your limit, always check to see if there is anything cheaper. If you are prepared to take a chance (not advisable in high season), many hotels are prepared to negotiate on the room price if they still have vacancies later in the day (after 6pm or so).

Shopping Districts & Malls

Florida Mall

The biggest shopping experience in Orlando, with 250 specialty stores anchored by outposts of the Saks Fifth Avenue, Sears, J. C. Penney, Burdines and Dillard's department stores. Popular brand-name fashion boutiques include Gap, The Limited, Benetton and Banana Republic, and there is a well-stocked Warner Bros Studio Store (► 106). If all that shopping works up a hunger, take your pick from 30 refreshment and dining options in the Food Court. Located at Sand Lake Road and the Florida Turnpike, its placement on the route to and from Orlando International Airport makes it extremely popular with travelers.

✉ **8001 S Orange Blossom Trail/US441** ☎ **(407) 851 6255** 🚌 **Lynx #42**

Orlando

The Mall at Millenia

Orlando's latest shopping extravaganza boasting 150-plus fashion and specialist stores from Bang & Olufsen to Gucci via Gap, Neiman Marcus, and many eateries.

✉ **4200 Conroy Road (at I-4)** ☎ **(407) 363 3555**

The Mercado

A landmark tower sprouts above this Mediterranean-style marketplace. Some 60 specialty shops and restaurants set around an open-air courtyard with live entertainment.

✉ **8445 International Drive** ☎ **(407) 345 9337** 🚌 **I-Ride, Lynx #42**

Orlando Fashion Square Mall

A bit far from the tourist-beaten trail in east Orlando. Among the 165 boutiques and shops are branches of Sears, Burdines and J. C. Penney department stores.

✉ **3201 E Colonial Drive/SR50** ☎ **(407) 896 1131**

Pointe*Orlando

Upscale shopping and entertainment complex. Mega book and music stores, plus a multi-screen movie theater, restaurants and sidewalk vendors.

✉ **9101 International Drive** ☎ **(407) 248 2838** 🚌 **I-Ride, Lynx #42**

Around Orlando

Kissimmee

Old Town Kissimmee

Around 70 souvenir stores, boutiques and gift shops, plus restaurants and amusement rides (► 60). Popular with tourists.

✉ **5770 W Irlo Bronson Memorial Highway/US192** ☎ **(407) 396 4888**

Winter Park

Park Avenue

An attractive downtown shopping district in a north Orlando suburb. Assorted boutiques, galleries, gifts and restaurants (► 66).

✉ **Park Avenue (at New York Avenue)** ☎ **(407) 644 8281**

Winter Park Village

A few blocks from the upscale Park Avenue, this manufactured and middle-class area is a pleasing recreation of a Main Street shopping village; complete with sidewalk cafes, bookstores, boutiques, furniture stores and a multi-screen movie theater.

✉ **500 Orlando Avenue**

Walt Disney World Resort and Lake Buena Vista

Crossroads at Lake Buena Vista

Small shopping and dining complex at the entrance to Walt Disney World, plus a supermarket. If you're staying at a Disney property, this is the closest option.

✉ **12541 SR535 (opposite Hotel Plaza Boulevard)** ☎ **(407) 425 9700**

Downtown Disney Marketplace

A fun place to shop and catch the breeze off the lake. Souvenirs, resortwear and World of Disney, the biggest Disney merchandise store in the world (► 106). Also eateries and boat hire from Cap'n Jack's Marina.

✉ **Buena Vista Drive** ☎ **(407) 828 3858**

Discount Outlets & Bargain Stores

Orlando

Belz Designer Outlet Centre

Just south of Belz (▶ below), designer fashion bargains from Esprit, DKNY, Off 5th-Saks Fifth Avenue, and others. Also Fila sportswear, china from Villeroy & Boch, jewelry and household appliances.

 5211 International Drive ☎ (407) 352 9611 🚊 I-Ride, Lynx #8, 42

Belz Factory Outlet World

Two full-scale malls and four annexes containing 170-plus outlet stores selling cut-price clothing, footwear, sporting goods and accessories (▶ panel).

✉ 5401 W Oakridge Road ☎ (407) 352 9611 🚊 I-Ride, Lynx #8, 42

Orlando Premium Outlets

This Mediterranean village is the setting for 110 stores including Banana Republic, Polo Ralph Lauren, Tommy Hilfiger and Verdace. savings of 25–65 percent.

✉ 8200 Vineland Avenue ☎ (407) 238 7787 🚊 I-Ride

Sports Dominator, Inc.

Massive selection of sportswear, shoes and equipment from top names including Adidas, Head and Nike, with discounts of up to 50 percent on selected items.

✉ 6464 International Drive ☎ (407) 354 2100 🚊 I-Ride, Lynx #42

Around Orlando

Kissimmee

Kissimmee Value Outlet Shops

Mini factory-outlet mall with 30-plus stores, including Nike, Calvin Klein and Tommy Hilfiger, offering 25–75 percent discounts.

✉ 4673 West US192 ☎ (407) 396 8900

Sports Dominator, Inc.

A Kissimmee outlet for this well-stocked sports outfitters (▶ Orlando, above).

✉ 7550 W US192 ☎ (407) 397 4700

Osceola Flea & Farmers Market

Sprawling 900-booth flea market (Fri–Sun) specializing in souvenirs, dubious antiques and collectables. Also fresh local produce.

✉ 2801 E Irlo Bronson Memorial Highway/US192 ☎ (407) 846 2811

Sanford
Flea World

America's largest weekend market under one roof (Fri–Sun): 1,700 dealer booths and thousands of bargains on souvenirs, toys, household items and unbelievable tat.

✉ US17-92 (4 miles/6km southeast of I-4/Exit 50) ☎ (407) 330 1792

Walt Disney World Resort and Lake Buena Vista
Lake Buena Vista Factory Stores

Over 30 factory-direct outlet stores and a food court. Look out for 20–75 percent off retail prices from the likes of Reebok, Liz Claiborne, Lee and Wrangler jeans from the VF-Factory Outlet, and the OshKosh B'Gosh Superstore.

✉ 15591 S Apopka-Vineland Road/SR535 (2 miles/3km south of I-4/Exit 27) ☎ (407) 622 5644

Bargain Belz

Resembling a giant shopping theme park at the top of International Drive, Belz Factory Outlet World is a magnet for thrifty shoppers. Bargain-hunters will find discounts of up to 75 percent off retail prices on an enormous range of goods. Obviously, few items come that dramatically discounted, but there are considerable savings to be had on top brand products from Bally, Converse, Foot Locker, Guess?, Levi Strauss, OshKosh B'Gosh, Sunglass Hut, Van Heusen and many more.

Souvenirs

The Great Merchandise Heist

If theme park admission were not enough to lighten your wallet, dozens of alluring merchandise outlets make it easy to spend a second unscheduled fortune on souvenirs. One tip is to make a deal with children beforehand about what they can expect to take home (a T-shirt, a stuffed toy, a pair of Mickey Mouse ears etc) and stick to it. Visitors to Walt Disney World Resort can also save valuable sightseeing time by avoiding the theme park stores and visiting the one-stop World of Disney superstore.

Orlando
Bargain World

Huge selection of cut-price Disney, MGM and Florida souvenir T-shirts, sportswear, swimwear and beach accessories.

✉ **5454 International Drive** ☎ **(407) 351 0900** ✉ **8520 International Drive** ☎ **(407) 352 0214** 🚌 **I-Ride, Lynx #42**

Orlando International Airport

Don't despair if you're at the airport and suddenly remember you need an extra gift for someone back home. Each of the major theme parks (Disney, Universal, SeaWorld, Kennedy Space Center) has an annex store at OIA carrying their most popular souvenirs.

The Universal Studios Store

Toy and souvenir store packed with Universal merchandise from Woody Woodpecker pyjamas to cuddly Curious Georges.

✉ **Universal CityWalk, 6000 Universal Boulevard** ☎ **(407) 363 8000**

Around Orlando

Kissimmee
Bargain World

Two Kissimmee locations for Bargain World's discounted items (► Orlando above).

✉ **5781 W US192 (west of I-4)** ☎ **(407) 396 7778;** ✉ **7586 W US192 (east of I-4)** ☎ **(407) 396 7199**

Titusville/Merritt Island
Space Shop

Don't blow the entire souvenir budget on Disney, the Kennedy Space Center's souvenir shop is full of unusual mementoes. Astronaut food is a favorite, plus posters and T-shirts.

✉ **Kennedy Space Center, SR405** ☎ **(407) 452 2121**

Theme Park Outlets

Remaindered souvenir merchandise from Orlando's theme parks provides bargain (50–75 percent) pickings for canny shoppers.

✉ **Kissimmee Value Outlet Shops, 4673 W Irlo Bronson Memorial Highway/US192** ☎ **(407) 390 7803**

Walt Disney World Resort and Lake Buena Vista
The Art of Disney

The place to find Disney posters, animation art, glossy art books and children's story books. Also at Disney-MGM Studios.

✉ **Downtown Disney Marketplace, Buena Vista Drive** ☎ **(407) 828 3058**

Once Upon a Toy

16,000sq ft (1,486sq m) of Disney themed merchandise plus top toy marque Hasbro of Mr Potato man fame.

✉ **Downtown Disney Marketplace, Lane Buena Vista Drive** ☎ **(407) 934 7745**

World of Disney

The world's largest Disney superstore with just about the full range of Disney merchandise from adults and children's clothing to toys, jewelry and trinkets. Kids and kitsch-crazy adults can blow the entire budget on Minnie Mouse slippers and Tigger baby-gros (► panel).

✉ **Downtown Disney Marketplace, Buena Vista Drive** ☎ **(407) 828 3058**

Miscellaneous

Orlando
Sci-Fi City
The world's largest science fiction store is bursting at the seams with books, comics, games, figurines and T-shirts galore. Worth a trip for all you sci-fi buffs out there.
✉ 6006 E Colonial Drive
☎ (407) 282 2292

Sound Shop
Stock up on affordable sounds and entertainment from Sound Shop's catalogue of CDs, tapes, movie and music videos, and DVDs.
✉ Pointe*Orlando (suite 314), 9109 International Drive
☎ (407) 363 9882 🚌 I-Ride, Lynx #42

World of Denim
Stock up on the top US brand name jeans and casual wear from Levi's, Guess?, DKNY, No Fear and Timberland among others.
✉ 7623 International Drive
☎ (407) 351 5704 🚌 I-Ride, Lynx #42;
✉ 5210 W Irlo Bronson Memorial Highway, Kissimmee
☎ (407) 390 4561

Around Orlando

Cocoa Beach
Ron Jon Surf Shop
A local institution in this lively seaside town (➤ 68–9). Nine acres (3.5ha) of cool surfie beach gear, sand sculptures, board or in-line skate rental and café. Open 24 hours.
✉ 4151 N Atlantic Avenue/A1A (near junction with SR520)
☎ (407) 799 8888

Kissimmee
Shell World
Florida's oldest and largest retailer of seashells, coral and nautical knick-knacks: 50,000 shells from around the globe from less than a dollar to valuable collectables.
✉ 4727 W Irlo Bronson Memorial Highway/US192
☎ (407) 396 9000

Mount Dora
Renninger's Twin Markets
Mount Dora's antiques community is anchored by Renninger's Twin Markets, which features a side-by-side flea market and antiques market. Open each weekend you can start at the flea market for odds and ends and produce, and then head to the antiques market for goods of surprising diversity and quality.
☎ (352/383 8393)

Walt Disney World and Lake Buena Vista
Disney's Days of Christmas
It is 25 December all year round at this Christmassy store laden with yule-themed gifts and decorations. Mickey, Minnie, Winnie the Pooh and other favorite Disney characters are all dressed up and ready for the festivities.
✉ Downtown Disney Marketplace, Buena Vista Drive
☎ (407) 828 3058

Wyland Galleries of Florida
Marine paintings, sculpture and prints from one of the world's leading environmental artists famous for his giant "whaling wall murals."
✉ Disney's BoardWalk, 2101 N Epcot Resorts Boulevard
☎ (407) 560 8750

Antiquing
Antiques-fanciers will find a few browsing spots around Orlando. East of Kissimmee, almost a dozen small antiques and collectables stores gather around New York Avenue in downtown St. Cloud's quiet historic district. For more upscale pickings, try the smart antiques shops and galleries on Park Avenue in the prosperous Orlando suburb of Winter Park (➤ 66). But the best antiquing opportunity around is downtown Mount Dora (➤ 54).

Alternative Attractions

Theme Park Survival Tips

The chief rule is: don't overdo it. Tired, overwrought children are bad company, so tailor your stay to their energy levels. Rent a stroller so that young children can always hitch a ride, and take plenty of short breaks. Walt Disney World Resort or Universal Studio Escape guests staying close by might consider making an early start, returning to the hotel for a rest and a swim, and revisiting the park in the cool of the evening (get a handstamp to allow readmittance). Be warned: many of the thrill rides are limited to passengers measuring 44in (3ft 8in, or 1.12m) or more.

Orlando is all about children, but there are a few options other than the theme parks for younger visitors.

Orlando
Fun Spot Action Park

Multi-level, action-packed family attraction with go-karting, bumper cars and boats. Fairground-style rides such as the ferris wheel and kiddie rides. Also a massive games arcade. Caution: this can be very pricey.

✉ **5551 Del Verde Way (off International Drive)** ☎ **(407) 363 3867** 🕐 **Mon–Fri noon–midnight, Sat, Sun 10am–midnight**

Magical Midway

Another I-Drive family fun zone offering the full package of extreme go-kart tracks with corkscrew turns and wacky elevations, laser tag, bumper boats and cars, plus a giant slide.

✉ **Pointe*Orlando, 7001 International Drive** ☎ **(407) 370 5353** 🕐 **Sun–Thu 12–10, Fri 12–12** 🚌 **I-Ride, Lynx #42**

Orlando Science Center

A fun state-of-the-art science museum with dozens of interactive exhibits, film shows, a planetarium and 3-D laser shows (► 35).

✉ **777 E Princeton Street (I-4/Exit 85)** ☎ **(407) 514 2000 or 1-800 672 4386** 🕐 **Tue–Thu 9–5, Fri–Sat 9–9, Sun 12–5**

Skull Kingdom

Step through a giant skull into this haunting family attraction. Spooky, interactive exhibits augmented by live actors and special effects culminating in the Ghoulish Face Painting Gallery. Not recommended for under 8s.

✉ **5933 American Way (off International Drive)** ☎ **(407) 354 1564** 🕐 **Daily 12–2**

SkyVenture

Experience a skydiving thrill without the hassle of using a plane and a parachute as a huge blow dryer places you atop a column of air to keep you afloat like a real skydiver. Just off International Drive.

✉ **6805 Visitors Circle** ☎ **(407) 903 1150** 🕐 **Mon–Fri 2-midnight, Sat, Sun noon–midnight**

WonderWorks

A Spielberg-inspired interactive games attraction boasting 100-plus exhibits from earthquake and hurricane simulators to virtual hang-gliding and laser tag. A favorite is a design-your-own roller coaster site.

✉ **Pointe*Orlando, 9067 International Drive** ☎ **(407) 351 8800** 🕐 **Daily 9–midnight** 🚌 **I-Ride, Lynx #42**

Around Orlando

Clearwater Beach
Sea Screamer

A day trip from Orlando (approx 90 mins west via I-4), Clearwater is renowned for glorious beaches and dolphin cruises. Here the 73-ft (22-m), twin-turbo Sea Screamer (the world's biggest speedboat) combines a gentle harbor cruise with a blast out into the Gulf of Mexico that guarantees thrills, dolphin sightings and a probable drenching.

✉ **Clearwater Beach Marina** ☎ **(727) 447 7200** 🕐 **Spring–fall daily at noon, 2pm, 4pm; Jun–mid-Sep also 6pm**

Kissimmee

Green Meadows Petting Farm

Farmyard fun for young children with pony rides and lots of animals to meet and pet (▶ 55).

⊠ 1368 S Poinciana Boulevard ☎ (407) 846 0770 ⏱ Daily 9.30–5.30

The Ice Factory

This ice-skating center has two rinks and skating lessons. Skate rental and pro-shop, plus a children's play area, snack bar and video arcade.

⊠ 2221 Partin Settlement Road ☎ (407) 933 4259 ⏱ Daily 6am–midnight

Makinson Aquatic Center

A bargain alternative to the expensive water parks, this family pool is a great place to splash around, play on the scaled-down waterslide and lounge in the sun, all for only a couple of dollars.

⊠ 2204 Denn John Lane ☎ (407) 870 7665 ⏱ Late Mar–end Sep (check schedules). Closed Mon and winter

Pirate's Cove and Pirate's Island Adventure Golf

There are two 18-hole miniature golf courses with a buccaneering theme at each of these locations.

⊠ 4330 W Vine Street/US192 ☎ (407) 396 4660; ⊠ 2845 Florida Plaza Boulevard ☎ (407) 396 7484 ⏱ Daily 9am–11.30pm

Ocala

Don Garlits Museums

A popular outing for boy (or girl) racers—and their dads and mums. There's 46,000sq ft (4,273sq m) of automotive excellence from muscle cars, hot rods and race cars to vintage Fords and a motor racing hall of fame, presented by the king of drag racing.

⊠ 13700 SW 16th Avenue (55 miles (89km) N of Orlando) ☎ (352) 245 8661 ⏱ Daily 9–5

Juniper Creek Canoe Run

Great for older children. The 7-mile (11-km) canoe trail runs through the Ocala National Forest (▶ 62) and takes around four hours. Canoes can be rented in advance.

⊠ Juniper Springs Recreation Area, SR40 (22 miles/35km east of Silver Springs), Ocala National Forest ☎ (352) 625 2802 ⏱ Mon–Fri 9–noon, Sat, Sun 8–noon

Sanford

Central Florida Zoological Park

Animal encounters in a Florida woodland setting among the live oaks and Spanish moss. The residents include big cats, monkeys, birds and reptiles. There are picnic areas and an animal petting corner.

⊠ US17-92 (south of I-4/Exit 52 towards Sanford) ☎ (407) 323 4450 ⏱ Daily 9–5, except Thanksgiving and Christmas

Walt Disney World Resort and Lake Buena Vista

DisneyQuest

Five floors of state-of-the-art interactive adventures and virtual reality experiences for all ages. Dodge the realistic virtual dinosaurs, design a roller-coaster and "fly" Aladdin's magic carpet.

⊠ Downtown Disney West Side ☎ (407) 828 4600 ⏱ Daily 10.30am–midnight

Southern Belles at Cypress Gardens

Drifting around the floral displays at Cypress Gardens (▶ 18, 52), like errant extras from the set of *Gone With the Wind*, the park's ringleted and crinolined trademark Southern Belles are many a little girl's dream. Conversely, they are many a grown man's dream as well and accommodate the Rhett Butler wannabes by graciously posing for photos.

Beyond the Theme Parks

Citrus Country
Thousands of acres of Central Florida are planted with citrus trees, but visitors rarely get a chance to stop and explore the groves. During winter (Nov–end Apr), Ivey Groves Fresh Citrus, 2220 Boggy Creek Road, Kissimmee (☎ (407) 348 4757) offer daily orchard tours, and a chance to pick your own citrus fruits and sample free juices.

Around Orlando

Clermont
Laneridge Winery and Vineyards
Florida's largest and award-winning winery offers interesting tours and tastings of red, white, rosé and sparkling wines.
✉ 19239 US27 North ☎ (352) 394 8627 or 1-800 768 9463
◉ Mon–Sat 10–5, Sun 11–5

Seminole Lake Gliderport
From a grassy airstrip in the countryside of Orlando you can take a glider (sailplane) tour with Knut Kyenslie. Flying without an engine and soaring with the birds is certainly an undeniable, peaceful thrill.
✉ Highways 33 & 561
☎ (352) 394 5450 ◉ Daily, except Mon

Daytona
Daytona USA
Take a trip to the "World Center of Racing" visitor center at the famous Daytona Speedway. Racing memorabilia, excellent interactive displays and games, merchandise store and guided track tours.
✉ 1801 W International Speedway Boulevard/US92 (I-4/Exit 57, 50 miles (81km) E of Orlando) ☎ (386) 947 6800
◉ Daily 9–5

Kissimmee
Aquatic Wonders Boat Trips
Two-hour and half-day boat trips on Lake Tohopekaliga (► 61). Fishing trips, birding and sunset cruises.
✉ 101 E Lakeshore Boulevard
☎ (407) 846 2814
◉ Daily from 9am, by appointment

Boggy Creek Airboat Rides
Half-hour airboat trips into the Central Florida wetlands explore 10 miles (16km) of sawgrass and natural creeks looking for wildlife. Nighttime 'gator hunts by arrangement.
✉ East Lake Fish Camp, 3702 Big Bass Road (off Boggy Creek Road) ☎ (407) 348 4676
◉ Daily 9am–dusk

Kissimmee Rodeo
Kissimmee's cowboys and cowgirls compete in trials of skill and daring (► 60).
✉ Kissimmee Sports Arena, 958 S Hoagland Boulevard ☎ (407) 933 0020 ◉ Fri 8–10pm

Warbird Adventures, Inc.
Take to the skies in T-6/Harvard World War II fighter-trainer for an aerobatic thrill or gentle sightseeing flight.
✉ 233 N Hoagland Boulevard
☎ (407) 870 7366 or 1-800 386 1593 ◉ Daily 9–sunset

Walt Disney World Resort and Lake Buena Vista
Richard Petty Driving Experience
Ride with a pro or drive a 630hp NASCAR stock car down the backstretch at speeds of up to 145mph (234kph).
✉ Walt Disney Speedway
☎ (407) 939 0130 or 1-800 237 3889 ◉ Daily 8–5 (extended in summer)

Sanford
Rivership Romance
Riverboat lunch and Friday and Saturday night dinner-dance cruises on Lake Monroe and St. Johns River. Popular with an older crowd.
✉ 433 N Palmetto Avenue
☎ (407) 321 5091 or 1-800 423 7401 ◉ Daily 8.30–5.30

Sports

Fishing

Orlando

Bass Challenger Guide Services, Inc

Full- and half-day fishing trips with all equipment and transportation provided.

✉ PO Box 679155 ☎ (407) 273 8045 ⏲ Daily, by arrangement

Kissimmee

A #1 Bass Guide Service

Fully rigged bass boats and tackle for half-, full-day and nighttime fishing trips.

✉ PO Box 421257, Kissimmee ☎ (352) 394 3660 or 1-800 707 5463 ⏲ Daily, by arrangement

Golf

► 68–9.

Horse-riding

Orlando

Grand Cypress Equestrian Center

A wide variety of lessons and programs, English and Western trail rides at this up-market hotel resort.

✉ Grand Cypress Resort, One Grand Cypress Boulevard ☎ (407) 239 1981 or 1-800 835 7377 ⏲ Daily 8–5

Kissimmee

Horse World Riding Stables

Woodland trails for experienced and novice riders (► 108).

✉ 3705 S Poinciana Boulevard ☎ (407) 847 4343 ⏲ Daily from 9am

Walt Disney World Resort and Lake Buena Vista

Trailblaze Corral

Trail rides through the Fort Wilderness countryside (riders must be aged 9 or more). Also pony rides for little children. (► 90)

✉ Disney's Fort Wilderness Resort, 4510 N Fort Wilderness Trail ☎ (407) 939 7529 ⏲ Daily 10–5

Tennis

Orlando

Orlando Tennis Center

A good downtown budget option with 16 courts and good facilities.

✉ 649 W Livingstone Street ☎ (407) 246 2162 ⏲ Mon–Fri 8–10, Sat 8–8, Sun 8–6

Kissimmee

Orange Lake Country Club & Resort

Sixteen well-priced courts close to Disney; reservations are not always necessary.

✉ 8505 W Irlo Bronson Memorial Highway/US192 ☎ (407) 239 1050 ⏲ Daily

Walt Disney World Resort and Lake Buena Vista

Disney's Racquet Club

State-of-the-art clay courts, private and group lessons, tennis ball machines, or sign up at Players Without Partners.

✉ Disney's Contemporary Resort ☎ (407) 939 7529 ⏲ Daily

Watersports

Orlando

Buena Vista Water Sports/Dave's Ski School

Water-ski lessons, Jet Ski and competition ski boat rentals, and tube rides for groups (see panel). Reserve ahead.

✉ 13245 Lake Bryan Drive ☎ (407) 239 6939 ⏲ Daily

Watersports at Walt Disney World Resort

Walt Disney World Resort's numerous lakes and lagoons are ideal for messing about on the water. Most of the hotels have waterfrontage and marinas where guests can rent a variety of small sail boats, jet boats, watersprites and pedal boats. There is water-skiing from the Fort Wilderness marina, parasailing from the Contemporary Resort, and canoeing along scenic canals from the Fort Wilderness, Caribbean Beach, Dixie Landings and Port Orleans marinas.

Spectator Sports

Spring Training
While most of the country shivers in grim winter temperatures, sunny Central Florida is the ideal location for the nation's top baseball teams to get in shape for the forthcoming playing season. During Feburary and March, fans can catch friendly games and practice sessions from the Houston Astros at Kissimmee, and the Atlanta Braves at Disney's Wide World of Sports Complex. Elsewhere in Central Florida, the Detroit Tigers train at Lakeland and the Cleveland Indians at Winter Haven.

American Football

Orlando Predators
Aspiring local Arena Football League competitors. Check listings in the local papers for details of upcoming games.
✉ **TD Waterhouse Centre, 600 W Amelia Street** ☎ **(407) 648 4444**

Baseball

Orlando
Atlanta Braves
At Disney's Wide World of Sports Complex, the Braves play their spring training games against other pro teams in a brand-new, old-fashioned stadium where you can spread out a blanket on the lawn and watch professional players up close.
✉ **Walt Disney World Resort** ☎ **(407) 939 1500**

Kissimmee
Osceola County Stadium & Sports Complex
Spring training home of the Houston Astros (➤ panel) and host to many amateur and professional baseball events throughout the year.
✉ **1000 Bill Beck Boulevard (off E US192)** ☎ **(407) 933 5400**

Basketball

Orlando Magic
Downtown TD Waterhouse Centre is home to the local Eastern Division NBA contenders when they are in town. Season Oct to Apr/May, reservations advised.
✉ **TD Waterhouse Centre, 600 W Amelia Street** ☎ **(407) 896 2442 or 1-800 338 0005**
❓ **Tickets from Ticketmaster** ☎ **1-800 4NBA TIX**

Orlando Miracle
When the Magic are taking a summer break, the Miracle women's NBA professionals provide fun family sporting entertainment.
✉ **TD Waterhouse Centre, 600 W Amelia Street** ☎ **(407) 916 9622**

Golf

PGA Events
Home to 30 PGA Tour pros and 11 LPGA pros, Orlando is Florida's golfing capital. Local courses host two annual PGA events: in Mar, the Bay Hill Invitational is played at the Arnold Palmer Golf Academy, 9000 Bay Hill Boulevard, Orlando ☎ (407) 876 5362; in Oct, Disney offer a million-dollar purse for the National Car Rental Golf Classic ☎ (407) 939 4653.

Motor Racing

Daytona International Speedway
Home to the famous Daytona 500 and Speed Weeks race program (Feb), plus the Bike Week (Mar) and Biketoberfest (Oct) motorcyle events.
✉ **1801 W International Speedway Boulevard** ☎ **(386) 253 RACE (7223)**

Sports Complex

Disney's Wide World of Sports Complex
Disney's spectacular 200-acre (81-ha) sporting venue boasts world-class facilities for more than 30 sports, a speedway, and hosts national and international events.
✉ **Lake Buena Vista** ☎ **(407) 939 1500** 🕐 **Daily 10–5 and special events**

Dinner Shows

Orlando
Dolly Parton's Dixie Stampede
The legendary country siren lent her name to promote this down-home dinner show near Disney. The theme is North vs. South showdown centered around horse racing, stunts and lots of music. Great southern cooking—that you'll eat minus untensils.

✉ **8251 Vineland Avenue**
☎ **(866) 443 4943;**
www.dixiestampede.com
⊙ **Check website for schedule**

Pirate's Dinner Adventure
Yo ho ho and a suitably piratical dinner show with a motley crew of entertainers, stunt men and a post-show Buccaneer Bash.

✉ **6400 Carrier Drive (off International Drive)** ☎ **(407) 248 0590 or 1-800 866 2469**
⊙ **Nightly**

Sleuths Mystery Dinner Shows
Solve a whodunnit between courses at this small dinner attraction. Entertaining action with a comedy angle and plenty of red herrings, but dinner is a rather long-winded affair for those attending the second show.

✉ **7508 Universal Boulevard**
☎ **(407) 363 1985** ⊙ **Nightly**

Around Orlando
Kissimmee
Arabian Nights
A spectacular equestrian dinner attraction, with over $5 million-worth of prime horseflesh and enough glitz to rival Las Vegas. Good family entertainment and a real treat for horse-mad kids.

✉ **6225 W Irlo Bronson**

Memorial Highway/US192 (GM 8) ☎ **(407) 239 9223 or 1-800 553 6116** ⊙ **Nightly**

Capone's
An intimate 1930s speakeasy is the setting for this gangsters-and-molls comedy musical show. The small cast throws itself into the dance numbers with enthusiasm.

✉ **4740 W Irlo Bronson Memorial Highway/US192 (GM 12.5)** ☎ **(407) 397 2378 or 1-800 220 8428** ⊙ **Nightly**

Medieval Times
An evening of medieval spectator sports as dashing knights take part in action-packed horseback games of skill and daring, jousting and sword fights.

✉ **4510 W Irlo Bronson Memorial Highway/US192 (GM 14.5)** ☎ **(407) 396 2900 or 1-888 935 6878** ⊙ **Nightly**

Walt Disney World Resort and Lake Buena Vista
Disney's Spirit of Aloha
Open-air tropical feast at the Polynesian Resort where you dine on foods inspired by the South Seas: lanai-roasted chicken and BBQ ribs in a backyard beachside cabana. Hula lessons included.

✉ **Disney's Polynesian Resort, 1600 Seven Seas Drive** ☎ **(407) 939 3463** ⊙ **Nightly**

Hoop-Dee Doo Musical Revue
Popular Disney country-style hoe-down with sing-along tunes and a good all-you-can-eat barbecue. Three shows nightly; reserve ahead.

✉ **Disney's Fort Wilderness Resort, 4510 N Fort Wilderness Trail** ☎ **(407) 939 3463**
⊙ **Nightly**

The Bottom Line
Dinner shows are enormously popular, but can be expensive. The average price for dinner (including unlimited wine, beer and non-alcoholic drinks) and a show is around $45 per adult. And, let's be honest, dinner theaters are not in the business of gourmet dining. Food is generally plentiful, but indifferent, tepid and occasionally inedible. The trick is to ignore promising menu descriptions and pick out the show most suited to your group of family or friends.

Live Music, Entertainment & Sports Bars

Stargazing

For a rather less conventional night out, the Orlando Science Center (➤ 35) invites stargazers to survey the universe through Florida's largest publicly accessible refractor telescope on Friday and Saturday evenings. On the same evenings, the Center also features laser light shows to rock music soundtracks and 3-D special effects in the world's largest Digistar II Planetarium, the CineDome (information, ☎ (407) 514 2114 or 1-888 672 4386).

Orlando

Friday's Front Row Sports Grill

Satellite sporting entertainment on tap, all-American menu and games room.

✉ 8126 International Drive
☎ (407) 363 1414 🕐 Daily until 2am 🚌 I-Ride, Lynx #42

Hard Rock Live

A huge venue for live concerts, it's adjacent to the world's largest Hard Rock restaurant. There's a large lobby area with a full bar if you want a drink or the music's loud and you need to escape.

✉ Universal CityWalk ☎ (407) 351 5483; www.hardrock.com 🕐 Check schedules

Peacock Room

Leaning toward upscale with live jazz, a martini bar and a DJ. Winner of several local awards for their drinks and art shows.

✉ 1321 N Mills Avenue
☎ (407) 228 0048 🕐 Nightly until 2am

Pointe*Orlando

After dark entertainment at a choice of restaurants, clubs and a multi-screen cinema with an IMAX 3-D theater.

✉ 9101 International Drive (at Republic Drive) ☎ (407) 248 2838 🕐 Daily 🚌 I-Ride, Lynx #42

Sak Comedy Lab

Best live comedy venue in Orlando. Award-winning improvisational shows at this downtown location.

✉ 380 W Amelia Street
☎ (407) 648 0001 🕐 Check schedules

Universal CityWalk

Universal's dining and entertainment zone includes the Motown Café, CityJazz, Bob Marley—A Tribute to Freedom, the NASCAR café and Pat O'Brien's Irish bar, as well as a Hard Rock Café and a Hard Rock Live music venue.

✉ Universal Orlando, 1000 Universal Boulevard ☎ (407) 363 8000 🕐 Nightly

Walt Disney World Resort and Lake Buena Vista

Cirque du Soleil-La Nouba

Created exclusively for Walt Disney World by the world-renowned Cirque du Soleil, La Nouba is more an experience than a show. Avant-garde choreography meets Broadway spectacle and fantastical sets. There is live music, breathtaking circus skills and the requsite dose of whimsy as cast captivate audiences of all ages.

✉ Downtown Disney West Side ☎ (407) 934 6110
🕐 Tue–Sat at 6pm and 9pm

Disney's BoardWalk

Microbrewery, duelling and grand pianos at Jellyrolls, the ESPN Club Sports Bar and assorted shops, vendors and activities.

✉ 2101 N Epcot Resorts Boulevard ☎ (407) 939 5100 🕐 Nightly

House of Blues

Restaurant-cum-live music venue featuring blues, R&B, jazz and country. Occasional top name performers (check schedules).

✉ Downtown Disney West Side ☎ (407) 934 2583
🕐 Mon–Thu 7.30–2am, Fri–Sat 8–2am, Sun 9–3am

Nightclubs & Discotheques

Orlando

Backstage at the Rosen
Live bands and DJs playing hits from the 70s through to the present day at I-Drive's only nightclub without a cover charge.

✉ **Clarion Plaza Hotel, 9700 International Drive** ☎ **(407) 996 9700 ext 1684** ⏰ **Nightly until 2am** 🚌 I-Ride, Lynx #42

The Club at Firestone
One of Orlando's most popular gay bars always throbbing with loud music; Latin, hip-hop, reggae and techno-pop disco.

✉ **578 N Orange Avenue** ☎ **(407) 872 0066** ⏰ **Nightly until 3am**

Dragon Room
Dress sharp for this downtown club where special nights include complimentary cocktail receptions, plus DJ nights with hip-hop, R&B and pop music from the 80s and up.

✉ **25 W Church Street** ☎ **(407) 843 8600** ⏰ **Nightly until 3am**

The Groove
Featuring state-of-the-art sound and lighting, DJ Club and Dance mixes plus occasional live shows. Three of the seven bars are themed "mood" rooms where guests can chat over cocktails.

✉ **Universal CityWalk, 6000 Universal Boulevard** ☎ **(407) 363 8000** ⏰ **Nightly until 2am**

Matrix and Metropolis
Orlando's largest dance floor, a multi-million dollar light show and changing menu of DJ selected Top 40, techno, Eurotrance and breakout sounds all conveniently located on I-Drive. Good for groups.

✉ **Pointe* Orlando, 9101 International Drive, Suite 2300** ☎ **(407) 370 3700** ⏰ **Nightly until 3am** 🚌 I-Ride, Lynx #42

Tabu
A downtown venue for clubbers who prefer a more sophisticated SoBe (that's South Beach, Miami) atmosphere. State-of-the-art sound system, sushi bar, private VIP rooms with views of the dance floor on the upper level. Sunday night is Latin night. Min. age 21.

✉ **46 N Orange Avenue** ☎ **(407) 648 8363** ⏰ **Tue–Sat until 3am and Sun**

Around Orlando

Walt Disney World Resort and Lake Buena Vista

Laughing Kookaburra Good Time Bar
Popular and often very crowded hotel nightclub with a surprisingly small dance floor. There is live music, contemporary chart hits, speciality cocktails and a good party atmosphere.

✉ **Wyndham Palace Resort & Spa, 1900 Buena Vista Drive** ☎ **(407) 827 3722** ⏰ **Nightly until 2am**

Pleasure Island
Dedicated to a certain kind of hedonism, Pleasure Island has three discos (8Trax, Mannequins and the Rock-n-Roll Beach Club) and four clubs, including comedy and country and western venues, all crammed into Disney's top nighttime entertainment complex (▶ 89).

✉ **Downtown Disney, E Buena Vista Drive** ☎ **(407) 934 7781** ⏰ **Nightly until 2am**

It's the Law
Most discotheques and clubs admit under 18s as long as they are accompanied by an adult, though some insist on a minimum age of 21. Florida law prohibits the purchase or consumption of alcohol by anyone under 21. IDs are checked frequently, so any youthful-looking adults would be well advised to carry a passport or similar form of ID showing proof of their age. Everybody (regardless of seniority) must provide proof of age for admission to Pleasure Island.

What's on When

January
Capital One Bowl: nationally televised college football game on New Year's Day.

February
International Carillon Festival: carillon concerts at Bok Tower Gardens.
Silver Spurs Rodeo: major event on the Professional Rodeo Cowboys Association circuit held in Kissimmee.
Daytona Speed Weeks: the Daytona 500 and more.

March
Cypress Gardens Spring Flower Festival: award-winning floral displays (until May).
Florida Strawberry Festival: Held in Plant City (between Orlando and Tampa), this is a hugely popular event with country music, agricultural shows and fair rides.
Kissimmee Bluegrass Festival: week-long toe-tapping music event.
Winter Park Sidewalk Arts Festival: long weekend of art, food, music and activities.
Pro Water Ski Tour and Wakeboard Series: waterbatics at the Orlando Water Sports Complex.

April
Epcot International Flower & Garden Festival: garden and greenhouse tours, demonstrations and displays.

May
Zellwood Sweet Corn Festival: 200,000 corn on the cobs get consumed over the weekend at this family event.

June
Florida Film Festival: full-length movies, documentaries and shorts from around the world.
Wet 'n' Wild Summer Nights: Start of summer late night season featuring live entertainment.

July
Lake Eola Fireworks at the Fountain: Orlando celebrates the Fourth of July with games, activities and fireworks in Lake Eola Park.

October
National Car Rental Golf Classic at Walt Disney World Resort: top golfers gather for this annual PGA Tour event.
Halloween: special events at Cypress Gardens and Universal Orlando's Islands of Adventure.
Silver Spurs Rodeo: the cowboys are back in Kissimmee.

November
Orlando Magic Season Opener: the Magic open the basketball season.
Cypress Gardens Mum (Chrysanthemum) Festival: 2.5 million blooms in spectacular displays.
Annual Festival of the Masters: art show at Downtown Disney.

December
Cypress Gardens Poinsettia Festival & Garden of Lights: 400,000 lights and 40,000 poinsettias for Christmas.
Mickey's Very Merry Christmas Party: celebrations at Magic Kingdom.
Christmas in the Park: exhibition of Tiffany glass with seasonal music in downtown Winter Park.
SeaWorld Orlando's Rockin' Holiday Nights New Year's Eve New Year's Eve celebrations.

Practical Matters

Above: *Taxi driver*
Right: *Monument to the States, Kissimmee*

117

TIME DIFFERENCES

GMT	Orlando	Germany	USA (NY)	Netherlands	Spain
12 noon	7am	1pm	7am	1pm	1pm
	←	→	←	→	→

BEFORE YOU GO

WHAT YOU NEED

● Required ○ Suggested ▲ Not required	Some countries require a passport to remain valid for a minimum period (usually at least six months) beyond the date of entry—contact their consulate or embassy or your travel agent for details.	UK	Germany	USA	Netherlands	Spain
Passport (valid for six months from date of entry)/National Identity Card		●	●	▲	●	●
Visa (Waiver form to be completed. Regulations change, please check)		▲	▲	▲	▲	▲
Onward or Return Ticket		●	●	▲	●	●
Health Inoculations (tetanus)		○	○	○	○	○
Health Documentation (reciprocal agreement) (➤ 123, Health)		▲	▲	▲	▲	▲
Travel Insurance		●	●	▲	●	●
Driving Licence (national or International Driving Permit)		●	●	●	●	●
Car Insurance Certificate		○	○	●	○	○
Car Registration Document		●	●	●	●	●

WHEN TO GO

Orlando

🟥 High season

⬜ Low season

22°C	23°C	25°C	27°C	27°C	30°C	32°C	32°C	30°C	28°C	25°C	22°C
JAN	FEB	MAR	APR	MAY	JUN	JUL	AUG	SEP	OCT	NOV	DEC
☀️	☁️	☁️	☀️	🌦️	☁️	☁️	☁️	🌦️	🌦️	☀️	☀️

🌧️ Wet   ☁️ Cloud   ☀️ Sun   🌦️ Sunshine & showers

TOURIST OFFICES

In the UK
Orlando/Kissimmee–St. Cloud Tourism Bureau, Inc. Visitor information and a free Orlando/Kissimmee pack of visitor guides to both areas and local map ☎ 020 7233 2305 or 0800 092 2352 (brochure line)

Complete and up-to-date details on attractions, dining, shopping, nightlife and recreation are available from www.orlandoinfo.com/uk and www.floridakiss.com

Visit Florida
For an *Official Florida Holiday Guide* ☎ 01737 644882. Visit Florida also provide a free phone tourist assistance hotline in Florida ☎ 1-800 656 8777. Further information from www.flausa.com

POLICE 911

FIRE 911

AMBULANCE 911

POLICE (NON EMERGENCY) 407/246 2414

WHEN YOU ARE THERE

ARRIVING

International carriers fly direct into Orlando Internatinal Airport, many services involve transfers to and from other US cities. The nearest alternative international gateway for scheduled flights is Tampa, 1½ hours from Orlando; several charter operators serve Orlando Sanford, 20 mins from Orlando.

Orlando International Airport

Miles to city center

9 miles (15km)

Journey times

🚌	N/A
🚐	45 minutes
🚗	30 minutes

Tampa International Airport

Miles to city center

85 miles (137km)

Journey times

🚌	2 hours
🚐	2 hours
🚗	90 minutes

MONEY

An unlimited amount of US dollars can be imported or exported, but amounts of over £10,000 must be reported to US Customs, as should similar amounts of gold. US dollars traveler's checks are accepted as cash in most places (not cabs) as are major credit cards.

Dollar bills come in 1,5, 10, 20, 50, 100 and 500 denominations. Note that all dollar bills are the same size and color—all greenbacks. One dollar is made up of 100 cents. Coins are of 1 cent (pennies), 5 cents (nickel), 10 cents (dime), 25 cents (quarter) and 1 dollar.

TIME

Orlando local time is Eastern Standard Time (the same as New York) which is five hours behind Greenwich Mean Time (GMT–5). Daylight saving applies, with clocks one hour ahead between April and October.

CUSTOMS

➔ **YES**

There are duty-free allowances for non-US residents over 21 years of age:

Alcohol: spirits (over 22% volume): 1L
Wine: 1L
Cigarettes: 200 *or*
Cigars: 50 *or*
Tobacco: 2kg
Duty-free gifts: $100 provided the stay in US is at least 72 hours and that gift exemption has not been claimed in the previous six months. There are no currency limits.

 NO

Meat or meat products, dairy products, fruits, seeds, drugs, lottery tickets or obscene publications.
Never carry a bag through Customs for anyone else.

CONSULATES/EMBASSIES

UK
☎ (407) 426 7855

Germany
☎ (202) 298 4320
(Washington)

Netherlands
☎ (407) 425 8000

Spain
☎ (305) 446 551
(Miami)

WHEN YOU ARE THERE

TOURIST OFFICES

Official Visitor Center
● 8723 International Drive,
  Gala Center (cnr Austrian
  Row)
  Orlando, Florida 32819
  ☎ (407) 363 5872
  🕐 All year 8am–7pm.

**Daytona Beach Area
Convention & Visitors Center**
● Visitor Information Center,
  Daytona USA, 1801 W
  International Speedway
  Boulevard
  ☎ (386) 253 8669 or 1-800
  854 1234

**Florida's Space Coast Office
of Tourism**
● 8810 Astronaut Boulevard,
  Cape Canaveral
  ☎ (321) 637 5483 or 1-800
  936 2326
Information desks at Kennedy
Space Center Visitor Complex

**Kissimmee—St. Cloud
Convention & Visitors
Bureau**
● Visitor Information Center,
  1925 E Irlo Bronson
  Memorial Highway/US192
  ☎ (407) 847 5000 or 1-800
  333 KISS 🕐 Daily 8–5

**Tampa Bay Visitor
Information Center**
● 615 Channelside Drive
  ☎ (813) 223 2752
  🕐 Daily 9–6

NATIONAL HOLIDAYS

J	F	M	A	M	J	J	A	S	O	N	D
2	1	(1)	(1)	1		1		1	1	2	1

Jan 1	New Year's Day
Jan (third Mon)	Martin Luther King Day
Feb (third Mon)	Washington's Birthday
Mar/Apr	Good Friday
May (last Mon)	Memorial Day
Jul 4	Independence Day
Sep (first Mon)	Labor Day
Oct (second Mon)	Columbus Day
Nov 11	Veterans' Day
Nov (fourth Thu)	Thanksgiving
Dec 25	Christmas Day

Boxing Day is not a public holiday in the US. Some
shops open on National Holidays.

OPENING HOURS

○ Shops	● Post Offices
● Offices	◐ Museums
● Banks	◐ Pharmacies

8am	9am	10am	NOON	2pm	3pm	4pm	5pm	6pm

☐ Day   ☐ Midday

☐ Evening

There are two all-night pharmacies: Ekered Drugs,
908 Lee Road, and Walgreen Drug Store, International
Drive (opposite Wet 'n' Wild). Some shops in malls
and on International Drive open until 9pm. Post
offices are few and far between; hotels are usually
helpful with postal matters. Banks, offices and post
offices close on Saturday. Opening times of theme
parks vary with seasonal demand. Opening times of
museums vary; check with individual museum. Some
museums are closed on Monday.

DRIVE ON THE RIGHT

LAVATORIES FREE

PUBLIC TRANSPORTATION

Air Orlando is a major domestic and an international airport. There are non-stop flights from about 70 different US destinations, and links to more than 100 cities worldwide. It is easily accessible and within 15 miles (24km) of major attractions, such as Walt Disney World Resort, and downtown Orlando. Airport ☎ (407) 825 2355.

Trains Amtrak trains serve Orlando with four daily trains originating in New York, and Miami, also stopping at Winter Park and Sanford, north of the city, and Kissimmee near Walt Disney World Resort. Amtrak offers an Auto Train overnight service with sleepers, which conveys passengers with their cars and vans, and runs daily between Lorton, Va and Sanford, Fl. For general information ☎ 1-800 872 7245 (toll-free).

Buses Greyhound lines serve Orlando from many centers in the US: within the metropolitan area local buses provide a good service, notably Mears Transportation, which serves the airport and most of Orlando's main attractions and hotels. Greyhound bus ☎ 1-800 231 2222. For excursions around the area and to the major attractions, tour companies offer diverse itineraries or can customize trips for groups.

Urban Transport Besides cab and limousine service to anywhere in the Greater Orlando area, the city's Lynx bus system provides economical public transportation around Orlando ☎ (407) 841 8240. Bus stops are marked with a "paw" print of a Lynx cat. The I-ride buses serve International Drive, with stops every 5–10 minutes ☎ (407) 248 9590. The stops are marked "I-RIDE" at each Lynx bus stop.

CAR RENTAL

Rates are very competitive. Take an unlimited mileage deal, collision damage waiver and adequate (more than minimal) insurance. There is a surcharge on drivers under 25 and the minimum age is often 21 (sometimes 25). Expect to pay by credit card.

CABS

Cabs are plentiful in Orlando, but they are not accustomed to being hailed down in the street. Hotels are the best places to find a cab. If money is no object, limousine transportation can be easily arranged through your hotel's guest services desk.

DRIVING

Speed limit on interstate highways **55–70mph/ 88–112kph**

Speed limits on main roads: **55mph/88kph**

Speed limits on urban roads: **20–30mph/32–48kph** All speed limits are strictly enforced.

Must be worn by drivers and front-seat passengers. Children under four must use child safety seats; older children must use a safety seat or seat belt.

Random breath-testing. Never drive under the influence of alcohol.

Fuel (*gasoline*), is cheaper in America than in Europe. It is sold in American gallons (five American gallons equal 18L), and comes in three grades, all unleaded. Many gas stations have automatic vending machines that accept notes and major credit cards.

If you break down pull over, raise the hood (bonnet), switch on the hazard lights, and call the rental company or the breakdown number, which should be displayed on or near the dashboard. For added security, several major rental car agencies (including Alamo, Avis and Hertz) are now offering clients the option to rent an in-car mobile phone.

CENTIMETRES
0 1 2 3 4 5 6 7 8

INCHES
0 1 2 3

PERSONAL SAFETY

Orlando is not generally a dangerous place but to help prevent crime and accidents:

- Never open your hotel room door unless you know who is there. If in doubt call hotel security.
- Place valuables in a safety deposit box.
- Always lock your front and/or patio doors when in the room and when leaving. Use the safety chain/lock for security.
- When driving, keep all car doors locked.
- Never approach alligators, they can outrun a man.

Police assistance:
☎ **911**
from any call box

TELEPHONES

There are telephones in hotel lobbies, drug stores, restaurants, garages and at the roadside. A local call costs 25 cents. Buy cards for long distance calls from the Official Visitors Center, some pharmacies and grocery stores. Dial "0" for the operator. "Collect" means reverse the charges.

International Dialling Codes

From Orlando (US) to:	
UK:	011 44
Ireland:	011 353
Australia:	011 61
Germany:	011 49
Netherlands:	011 31
Spain:	011 34

POST

Post offices in Orlando are few and far between. Stamps from vending machines are sold at a 25 percent premium; it is best to buy them at your hotel. The international postcard rate is 80 cents. Post offices are usually open Mon–Fri 9am–5pm, but many hotels and major attractions provide a post office service out of hours.

ELECTRICITY

The power supply is: 110/120 volts AC (60 cycles)

Type of socket: sockets take two-prong, flat-pin plugs.

Visitors should bring adaptors for their 3-pin and 2-round-pin plugs.

TIPS/GRATUITIES

Yes ✓   No ✕

It is useful to have plenty of small notes		
Hotels (chambermaid, doorman etc)	✓	$1
Restaurants (waiter, waitresses)	✓	15/20%
Bar Service	✓	15%
Cabs	✓	15%
Tour guides (discretionary)	✓	
Porters	✓	$1 per bag
Hairdressers	✓	15%
Lavatories	✕	

PHOTOGRAPHY

What to photograph: Orlando and its nearby theme parks are great places to take photographs. There are plenty of opportunities for classic Disney shots, as well as those of natural flora and fauna.

When to photograph: The hot summer months can be very humid and may affect photography. The best time of day to photograph is between 1 and 6pm.

Where to buy film: All types of film and photo processing are freely available in drugstores, theme parks etc but it is cheaper to take your own film.

HEALTH

Insurance
Medical insurance cover of at least $1,000,000 unlimited cover is strongly recommended, as medical bills can be astronomical and treatment may be withheld if you have no evidence of means to pay.

Dental Services
Your medical insurance cover should include dental treatment, which is readily available, but expensive. Have a check up before you go. Dental referral telephone numbers are in the Yellow Pages telephone directory or ask at the desk of your hotel.

Sun Advice
By far the most common source of ill health in Florida is too much sun. Orlando in summer is very hot and humid and the sun is strong all year round. Use a sunscreen, wear a hat outdoors and ensure that everyone drinks plenty of fluids.

Drugs
Medicines can be bought at drug stores, certain drugs generally available elsewhere require a prescription in the US. Acetaminophen is the US equivalent of paracetamol. Take an insect repellent including Deet and cover up after dark, to avoid being bitten by mosquitoes.

Safe Water
Restaurants usually provide a jug of iced water. Drinking unboiled water from taps is safe but not always very pleasant. Mineral water is inexpensive and readily available.

CONCESSIONS

Students/Youths Most concessions at major theme parks apply to children aged 3–9, but some sights and attractions offer special admission prices to bona fide students. There are also concessionary rail fares (International Student Identity Card required as proof).

Senior Citizens (Seniors) Over three million mature travelers visit Orlando each year, in addition to the "Senior" permanent residents, and many special discounts are available to those over 55. Members of the American Association of Retired Persons, over 50 (AARPs) are eligible (with ID) for discounts on accommodations, meals, car rental, transportation and many attractions in the Orlando area.

CLOTHING SIZES

Orlando (USA)	UK	Rest of Europe		
36	36	46		
38	38	48		
40	40	50		Suits
42	42	52		
44	44	54		
46	46	56		
8	7	41		
8.5	7.5	42		
9.5	8.5	43		Shoes
10.5	9.5	44		
11.5	10.5	45		
12	11	46		
14.5	14.5	37		
15	15	38		
15.5	15.5	39/40		Shirts
16	16	41		
16.5	16.5	42		
17	17	43		
6	8	34		
8	10	36		
10	12	38		Dresses
12	14	40		
14	16	42		
16	18	44		
6	4.5	38		
6.5	5	38		
7	5.5	39		Shoes
7.5	6	39		
8	6.5	40		
8.5	7	41		

WHEN DEPARTING

- Check airport terminal number (there are three terminals) and allow plenty of time to get there and hand in any rental car.
- Arrive at check-in at least two hours before departure time.
- US Customs are strict. There are no departure taxes but ensure that you have all necessary documentation and that you are not contravening US Customs regulations.

LANGUAGE

The official language of the USA is English, and, given that one third of all overseas visitors come from the UK, Orlando natives have few problems coping with British accents and dialects. Spanish is also widely spoken, as many workers in the hotel and catering industries are of Latin American origin.

Many English words have different meanings and below are some words in common usage where they differ from the English spoken in the UK:

holiday	*vacation*	tap	*faucet*
fortnight	*two weeks*	handbag	*purse*
ground floor	*first floor*	luggage	*baggage*
first floor	*second floor*	suitcase	*trunk*
second floor	*third floor*	hotel porter	*bellhop*
flat	*apartment*	chambermaid	*room maid*
lift	*elevator*	surname	*last name*
eiderdown	*comforter*	cupboard	*closet*

cheque	*check*	25 cent coin	*quarter*
traveller's cheque	*traveler's check*	banknote	*bill*
		banknote (colloquial)	*greenback*
1 cent coin	*penny*		
5 cent coin	*nickel*	dollar (colloquial)	*buck*
10 cent coin	*dime*	cashpoint	*automatic teller*

grilled	*broiled*	biscuit	*cookie*
frankfurter	*frank*	scone	*biscuit*
prawns	*shrimp*	sorbet	*sherbet*
aubergine	*eggplant*	jelly	*jello*
courgette	*zucchini*	jam	*jelly*
maize	*corn*	confectionery	*candy*
chips (potato)	*fries*	spirit	*liquor*
crisps (potato)	*chips*	soft drink	*soda*

car	*automobile*	petrol	*gas, gasoline*
bonnet (of car)	*hood*	railway	*railroad*
boot (of car)	*trunk*	tram	*streetcar*
repair	*fix*	underground	*subway*
caravan	*trailer*	platform	*track*
lorry	*truck*	buffer	*bumper*
motorway	*freeway*	single ticket	*one-way ticket*
main road	*highway*	return ticket	*round-trip ticket*

shop	*store*	policeman	*cop*
chemist (shop)	*drugstore*	post	*mail*
cinema	*movie theater*	post code	*zip code*
film	*movie*	ring up, telephone	*call*
pavement	*sidewalk*		
subway	*underpass*	long-distance call	*trunk call*
toilet	*rest room*		
trousers	*pants*	autumn	*fall*
nappy	*diaper*	gangway	*aisle*
glasses	*eyeglasses*	car park	*parking lot*

INDEX

Acknowledgements
The Automobile Assocation wishes to thank the following libraries and organizations for their assistance in the preparation of this book:

BUSCH ENTERTAINMENT CORP 27a, 48a, 50; CONGO RIVER, KISSIMMEE 53; DISCOVERY COVE 18, 30/1, KENNEDY SPACE CENTER 11; KISSIMMEE & ST CLOUD C & VB 55; LEU GARDENS 13; MARY EVANS PICTURE LIBRARY 10, 14; MRI BANKER'S GUIDE TO FOREIGN CURRENCY 119; NATURE PHOTOGRAPHERS 61 (P R Sterry); ORLANDO & ORANGE COUNTY C & VB 7a, 34, PICTURES COLOUR LIBRARY 8b, 22; RIPLEY'S BELIEVE IT OR NOT! 35; SPECTRUM COLOUR LIBRARY 16, 27b, 48b, 49; SEA WORLD 15a, 38/9a, 38/9b; UNIVERSAL STUDIOS 26, 41a; THE WALT DISNEY CO. 25, 70, 73, 74/5, 76/7, 78/9, 80, 82/3, 84/5, 87, 89, 90; WET N' WILD 1

The remaining photographs are held in the Association's own library (**AA PHOTO LIBRARY**) and were taken by Tony Souter, with the exception of the following:
P Bennett 7b, 9b, 12a, 12b, 15b, 20, 21, 23, 47, 51, 60, 62, 63, 66, 117a, 117b; J Davison 13.
The author would like to thank Jayne Teleska Behrle, Orlando-Orange County Convention and Visitors Bureau, Inc; Hayley Busse, Orlando-Orange County Convention and Visitors Bureau, UK; Larry White, Kissimmee-St. Cloud Convention and Visitors Bureau, USA; Sarah Handy, Kissimmee-St Cloud Convention and Visitors Bureau, UK; and Joyce Taylor, Walt Disney Attractions, UK.

This book makes reference to various Disney copyrighted characters, trademarks, marks and registered marks owned by The Walt Disney Company and Disney Enterprises, Inc.

Contributors
Copy editor: Nia Williams   Page Layout: Barfoot Design   Verifier: Paul Murphy
Researcher (Practical Matters): Lesley Allard   Indexer: Marie Lorimer
Revision management: Apostrophe S Limited

Dear Essential Traveller

Your comments, opinions and recommendations are very important to us. So please help us to improve our travel guides by taking a few minutes to complete this simple questionnaire.

You do not need a stamp (unless posted outside the UK). If you do not want to cut this page from your guide, then photocopy it or write your answers on a plain sheet of paper.

Send to: **The Editor, AA World Travel Guides, FREEPOST SCE 4598, Basingstoke RG21 4GY.**

Your recommendations...

We always encourage readers' recommendations for restaurants, nightlife or shopping – if your recommendation is used in the next edition of the guide, we will send you a *FREE* AA *Essential* **Guide** of your choice. Please state below the establishment name, location and your reasons for recommending it.

_____

_____

_____

_____

Please send me **AA *Essential*** _____

About this guide...

Which title did you buy?

AA *Essential* _____

Where did you buy it?_____

When? m m / y y

Why did you choose an AA *Essential* Guide? _____

_____

_____

_____

_____

Did this guide meet your expectations?

Exceeded ☐   Met all ☐   Met most ☐   Fell below ☐

Please give your reasons_____

_____

_____

_____

continued on next page...

Were there any aspects of this guide that you particularly liked? _____

_____

_____

Is there anything we could have done better? _____

_____

_____

About you...

Name (*Mr/Mrs/Ms*) _____

Address _____

_____

_____ Postcode _____

Daytime tel nos _____

Please only give us your mobile phone number if you wish to hear from us
about other products and services from the AA and partners by text or mms.

Which age group are you in?
Under 25 ☐ 25–34 ☐ 35–44 ☐ 45–54 ☐ 55–64 ☐ 65+ ☐

How many trips do you make a year?
Less than one ☐ One ☐ Two ☐ Three or more ☐

Are you an AA member? Yes ☐ No ☐

About your trip...

When did you book? m m / y y   When did you travel? m m / y y
How long did you stay? _____
Was it for business or leisure? _____
Did you buy any other travel guides for your trip?
   If yes, which ones? _____

Thank you for taking the time to complete this questionnaire. Please send it to us as soon as
possible, and remember, you do not need a stamp (*unless posted outside the UK*).

Happy Holidays!

The information we hold about you will be used to provide the products and services requested
and for identification, account administration, analysis, and fraud/loss prevention purposes. More
details about how that information is used in our privacy statement, which you'll find under the
heading "Personal Information" in our terms and conditions and on our website: www.theAA.com.
Copies are also available from us by post, by contacting the Data Protection Manager at AA, Fanum
House, Basing View, Basingstoke, Hampshire RG21 4EA.

We may want to contact you about other products and services provided by us, or our partners (by
mail, telephone) but please tick the box if you DO NOT wish to hear about such products and
services from us by mail or telephone. ☐

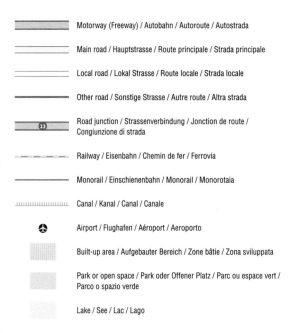

Motorway (Freeway) / Autobahn / Autoroute / Autostrada

Main road / Hauptstrasse / Route principale / Strada principale

Local road / Lokal Strasse / Route locale / Strada locale

Other road / Sonstige Strasse / Autre route / Altra strada

Road junction / Strassenverbindung / Jonction de route / Congiunzione di strada

Railway / Eisenbahn / Chemin de fer / Ferrovia

Monorail / Einschienenbahn / Monorail / Monorotaia

Canal / Kanal / Canal / Canale

Airport / Flughafen / Aéroport / Aeroporto

Built-up area / Aufgebauter Bereich / Zone bâtie / Zona sviluppata

Park or open space / Park oder Offener Platz / Parc ou espace vert / Parco o spazio verde

Lake / See / Lac / Lago

Maps © Global Mapping, Brackley, UK

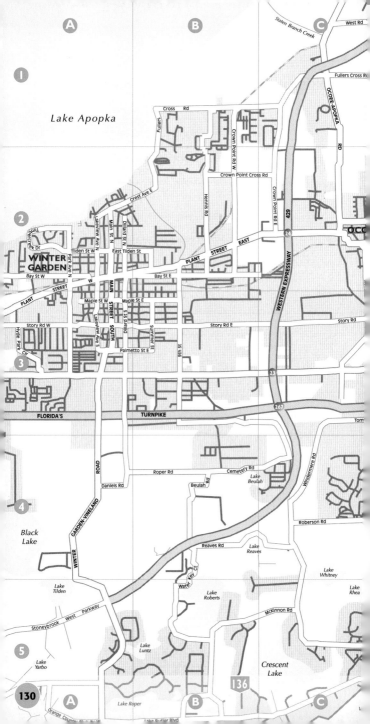

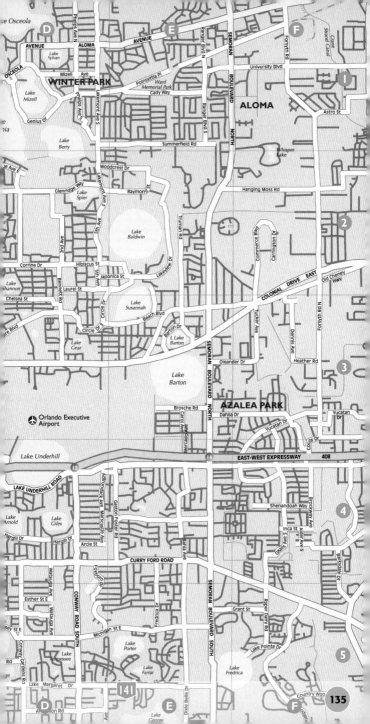

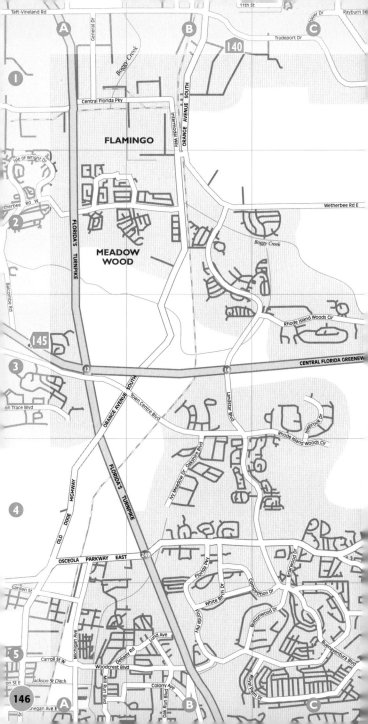

Taft-Vineland Rd

11th St

A   **B** 140   Tradeport Dr   **C** Rayburn St

General Dr

Boggy Creek

I

Central Florida Pky

ORANGE AVENUE SOUTH

New Intermodal

FLAMINGO

Isle of Wright Dr

therbee Rd W

Wetherbee Rd E

2

FLORIDA'S TURNPIKE

MEADOW WOOD

Boggy Creek

Balcombe Rd

Rhode Island Woods Cir

145

3

ORANGE AVENUE SOUTH

Town Centre Blvd

CENTRAL FLORIDA GREENEW

on Trace Blvd

12

14

Landstar Blvd

Rhode Island Woods Cir

Isikbrook Dr

4

OLD DIXIE HIGHWAY

FLORIDA'S TURNPIKE

Ivy Meadow Dr   Oakfield Blvd

OSCEOLA   PARKWAY   EAST   249

Florida Pky

Briarwood Dr

Garden st

White Birch Dr

Competition Dr

Buttonwood Dr

Florida Pky

Buenaventura Blvd

on St E

Lund Ave

5

Carroll St W

Ave urchison

DeBary Rd

Woodcrest Blvd

Jackson St Ditch

Mill Run Blvd

Colony Ave

Royal Palm Dr

negan Ave E

A   Oak Run Blvd   **B**   **C**

146

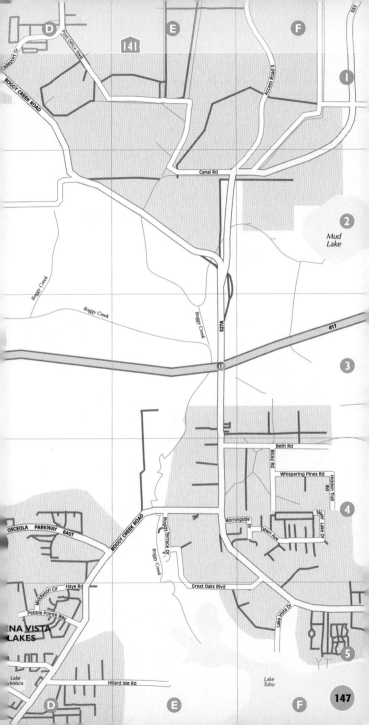

D
E
F
I

Lakeport Dr
Post Office Blvd
Access Road S
551

BOGGY CREEK ROAD

Mud
Lake
2

Canai Rd

Boggy Creek

Boggy Creek

Boggy Creek

527A

417

17

3

Beth Rd

Bicky Rd

Whispering Pines Rd

Hidden Trail Rd

4

Morningside Dr

Dawn Ave

Silver Lake Dr

OSCEOLA PARKWAY EAST

BOGGY CREEK ROAD

Boggy Terrace Dr

Boggy Creek

Great Oaks Blvd

Lake Vista Dr

McClosterton Cir

Haye Rd

Pebble Pointe Way

ENA VISTA LAKES

5

Lake Ventura

Hillard Isle Rd

Lake Toho

F

147

D
E
F

Day One

Day Two

Day Three

Day Four

Day Five

Day Six

Day Seven

STREET INDEX